GENERAL CONFERENCE ADDRESSES

GENERAL CONFERENCE ADDRESSES

———

JOURNAL EDITION
APRIL 2022

DESERET
BOOK

SALT LAKE CITY, UTAH

Book design © Deseret Book Company
Cover photo: andDraw/Getty Images
Interior photos: page 1, Witthaya Prasongsin/Getty Images; page 43, bgfoto/Getty Images; page 84, Brian A Jackson/Getty Images; page 109, ithinksky/Getty Images; page 148, Kami (Kuo, Jia-Wei)/Getty Images

April 2022 General Conference Addresses, Journal Edition by Deseret Book Company © by Intellectual Reserve, Inc.

DESERET BOOK is a registered trademark of Deseret Book Company.

Visit us at deseretbook.com

ISBN 978-1-63993-023-4

Printed in the United States of America
Sun Print Solutions, Salt Lake City, UT

10   9   8   7   6   5   4   3   2   1

CONTENTS

WOMEN'S SESSION

SUNDAY MORNING SESSION

SUNDAY AFTERNOON SESSION

SATURDAY MORNING SESSION

———

APRIL 2, 2022

PREACHING THE GOSPEL OF PEACE

PRESIDENT RUSSELL M. NELSON

President of The Church of Jesus Christ of Latter-day Saints

UKRAINE WAR :-(

My dear brothers and sisters, welcome to general conference! I have looked forward to this day with great anticipation. I pray for you *every day*. I have also prayed that this conference will be a time of spiritual rejuvenation for each one of you.

Since last conference, difficulties in the world have continued. The global pandemic still affects our lives. And now the world has been rocked by a conflict that is raining terror on millions of innocent men, women, and children.

Prophets have foreseen our day, when there would be wars and rumors of wars and when the whole earth would be in commotion.[1] As followers of Jesus Christ, we plead with leaders of nations to find peaceful resolutions to their differences. We call upon people everywhere to pray for those in need, to do what they can to help the distressed, and to seek the Lord's help in ending any major conflicts.

Brothers and sisters, the gospel of Jesus Christ has never been needed more than it is today. Contention violates everything the Savior stood for and taught. I love the Lord Jesus Christ and testify that His gospel is the *only* enduring solution for peace. His gospel is a gospel of peace.[2]

His gospel is the *only* answer when many in the world are stunned with fear.[3] This underscores the urgent need for us to follow the Lord's instruction to His disciples to "go . . . into *all* the world, and preach the gospel to *every* creature."[4] We have the sacred responsibility to share the power and peace of Jesus Christ with all who will listen and who will let God prevail in their lives.

Every person who has made covenants with God has promised to care about others and serve those in need. We can demonstrate faith in God and always be ready to respond to those who ask about "the hope that is in [us]."[5] Each of us has a role to play in the gathering of Israel.

Today I reaffirm strongly that the Lord has asked *every* worthy, able young man to prepare for and serve a mission. For Latter-day Saint young men, missionary service is a priesthood responsibility. You young men have been reserved for this time when the promised gathering of Israel is taking place. As you serve missions, you play a pivotal role in this unprecedented event!

For you young and able sisters, a mission is also a powerful, but *optional*, opportunity. We *love* sister missionaries and welcome them wholeheartedly. What you contribute to this work is magnificent! Pray to know if the Lord would have you serve a mission, and the Holy Ghost will respond to your heart and mind.

Dear young friends, you are each vital to the Lord. He has held you in reserve until now to help gather Israel. Your decision to serve a mission, whether a proselyting or a service mission, will bless you and many others. We also welcome senior couples to serve when their circumstances permit. Their efforts are simply irreplaceable.

All missionaries teach and testify of the Savior. The spiritual darkness in the world makes the light of Jesus Christ needed more than ever. Everyone deserves the chance to know about the restored gospel of Jesus Christ. Every person deserves to know where they can find the hope and peace that "[pass] all understanding."[6]

May this conference be a time of peace and spiritual feasting for you. May you seek and receive personal revelation during these sessions, I pray in the sacred name of Jesus Christ, amen.

Notes
1. See Doctrine and Covenants 88:91.
2. See Doctrine and Covenants 27:16.
3. See Luke 21:26.
4. Mark 16:15, emphasis added; see also Matthew 28:19.
5. 1 Peter 3:15.
6. Philippians 4:7.

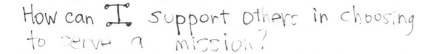

How can I support others in choosing to serve a mission?

MISSIONARY SERVICE BLESSED MY LIFE FOREVER

PRESIDENT M. RUSSELL BALLARD

Acting President of the Quorum of the Twelve Apostles

Thank you, President Nelson, for sharing again that counsel regarding missionary service.

Brothers and sisters, several years ago while I was speaking in general conference, the sight in my left eye was suddenly compromised by something called macular degeneration, which subsequently worsened and has left me without useful vision in that eye.

As I have dealt with this challenge, I am ever more thankful for other kinds of vision, including hindsight vision. As I have looked back over my life, I have been able to see certain experiences that made a significant difference. One of those experiences is how my full-time missionary service as a young man in England blessed my life and shaped my spiritual destiny.

I have reflected on how the economic challenges associated with the Great Depression in the 1930s led to an unfortunate turn for my parents and our family. My father became so involved in saving his automobile dealership and supporting a family during this difficult period that for a time my parents did not attend church.

Although we did not attend church services as a family, that did not prevent me from attending occasionally with my friends.

In those days, going on a mission was in the back of my mind, but it wasn't something I talked about with my parents.

While attending college, several friends and I decided to serve missions. Visiting with my bishop, I filled out my missionary application while my parents were out of town. When my parents returned, I surprised them with the news that I had been called to serve in Great Britain. I am grateful for their enthusiastic support of this decision and for good friends who helped me decide to serve.

My missionary service prepared me to be a better husband and father and to be successful in business. It also prepared me for a lifetime of service to the Lord in His Church.

In the April 1985 general conference, I was assigned to speak in the priesthood session. I directed my remarks to the young men. I spoke about preparing to serve as a missionary. I said, "Of all the training I have received in my Church assignments, none has been more important to me than the training I received as a nineteen-year-old elder serving a full-time mission."[1]

The Lord knows you. When you are serving your mission, you will have experiences that will help you come to know Him better. You will grow spiritually in serving Him. In His name, you will be sent on errands to serve others. He will give you experiences with promptings from the Holy Ghost. The Lord will authorize you to teach in His name. You can show Him that He can trust you and can rely on you.

Just over five months ago, Elder Jeffrey R. Holland and Elder Quentin L. Cook, who had also served as missionaries in the British Isles, joined me in visiting with members and missionaries in that beautiful land. While there, I reflected on my experiences as a young missionary. I testify that my mission is where I came to know that my Heavenly Father and my Savior, Jesus Christ, know and love me.

I was blessed to have two wonderful mission presidents, Selvoy J. Boyer and Stayner Richards, along with their dedicated companions, Gladys Boyer and Jane Richards. Looking back, I can see even more clearly that they trusted me and loved me. They taught me the gospel. They expected a lot from me. They gave me many challenging assignments and leadership responsibilities to help me to grow and prepare for a life of service.

I have also reflected on being called by President Spencer W. Kimball to preside over the Canada Toronto Mission with my dear wife, Barbara, and our children at our sides. President Kimball called us to serve in April 1974, shortly after he gave his inspired missionary message titled "When the World Will Be Converted."[2] In that message President Kimball explained his vision for how the gospel would be taken to all the world. He called for many more missionaries from around the world. He reminded us of the Lord's expectation "that every man should . . . lift a warning voice unto the inhabitants of the earth."[3] President Kimball's teaching about the expectation for young men to serve a mission became a topic of conversation in homes around the world. That expectation has not changed. I am grateful that President Russell M. Nelson also reaffirmed the Lord's expectation this morning.

It has been almost 10 years since President Thomas S. Monson announced the lowering of the missionary age for young men and young women.[4] In my view, a primary reason for this change was to give more of our youth the life-changing opportunity to serve as a missionary.

As an Apostle of the Lord Jesus Christ, I now call upon you young men—and those young women who desire to serve a mission—to begin right now to talk with your parents about serving a mission. I also invite you to talk with your friends about serving a mission, and if one of your friends is not sure about serving, encourage them to talk with their bishop.

Commit to yourselves and to your Heavenly Father that you will serve a mission and that from this time forward you will strive to keep your hearts, hands, and minds clean and worthy. I invite you to gain a solid testimony of the restored gospel of Jesus Christ.

Fathers and mothers of these wonderful youth, you have a vital role in this preparation process. Begin today to talk with your children about missionary service. We know that the family is the most profound influence in helping our young men and young women prepare.

If you are still in the age range for missionary service but have not served yet due to the pandemic or other reasons, I invite you to serve now. Talk to your bishop, and prepare to serve the Lord.

I encourage you bishops to help all young men and young women who are close to missionary age to prepare to serve, and I also encourage you bishops to identify those who are old enough but who have not yet served. Invite each young man to become a missionary, as well as each young woman who desires to serve.

To the missionaries currently serving, we thank you. Your mission has been during a worldwide pandemic. As a result, your mission experience has been unlike my mission experience or the experiences of any missionaries who served before 2020. I know it has not been easy. But even during these difficult times, the Lord has had a work for you to do, and you have done it wonderfully well. For example, you have used technology in new ways to find those who are ready to learn about the Restoration of the gospel of Jesus Christ. As you have served diligently and according to your abilities, I know that the Lord is pleased with your effort. I know that your service will bless your life.

When you are released from your mission, remember that you are not released from activity in the Church. Build upon the good habits you learned on your mission, continue to strengthen your testimony, work hard, pray, and be obedient to the Lord. Honor the covenants you have made. Continue to bless and serve others.

I pray that you young men and young women and your parents will see and know how missionary service will forever bless your life. May you know in your minds and feel in your hearts the power of the invitation the Lord gave to the great missionary sons of Mosiah. He said, "Go forth . . . and establish my word; yet ye shall be patient in long-suffering and afflictions, that ye may show forth good examples . . . in me, and I will make an instrument of thee in my hands unto the salvation of many souls."[5]

May God bless the youth of the Church to desire to prepare and serve Him is my humble prayer, which I offer this morning in the sacred name of the Lord Jesus Christ, amen.

Notes

1. M. Russell Ballard, "Prepare to Serve," *Ensign*, May 1985, 41.
2. See Spencer W. Kimball, "When the World Will Be Converted," *Ensign*, Oct. 1974, 2–14. This address was delivered on April 4, 1974, at a regional representatives' seminar.
3. Doctrine and Covenants 63:37.
4. See Thomas S. Monson, "Welcome to Conference," *Ensign* or *Liahona*, Nov. 2012, 4–5.
5. Alma 17:11.

WE ARE THE CHURCH OF JESUS CHRIST OF LATTER-DAY SAINTS

REYNA I. ABURTO
Second Counselor in the Relief Society General Presidency

After receiving an invitation to "come and see,"[1] I attended The Church of Jesus Christ of Latter-day Saints for the first time at the age of 26. I had recently separated from my first husband. I had a three-year-old boy. And I felt powerless with fear. When I entered the building, I was filled with warmth as I perceived the faith and joy of the people surrounding me. It was truly "a refuge from the storm."[2] Three weeks later, I made the baptismal covenant with Heavenly Father and started my journey as a disciple of Christ, although my life has not been perfect along that journey.

For me to receive those eternal blessings, many physical and spiritual elements had to be in place. The gospel of Jesus Christ had been restored and preached; that meetinghouse had been built and maintained; there was an ecclesiastical structure, from the prophet to local leaders; and a branch filled by covenant members was ready to embrace me and my son as we were brought to the Savior, "nourished by the good word of God,"[3] and given opportunities to serve.[4]

From the beginning, God has sought to gather and organize His children[5] "to bring to pass [our] immortality and eternal life."[6] With that purpose in mind, He has instructed us to build places of worship[7] where we receive knowledge and the ordinances of salvation and exaltation; make and keep covenants that bind us to Jesus Christ;[8] are endowed with "the power of godliness";[9] and gather together often to remember Jesus and strengthen each other in Him.[10] The Church organization and its buildings exist for our spiritual benefit. "The Church . . . is the scaffolding with which we build eternal families."[11]

While talking to a friend going through a difficult time, I asked how he was surviving financially. In tears, he replied that his bishop was helping him using fast-offering funds. He added, "I don't know where my family and I would be if it wasn't for the Church." I replied, "The Church is the *members*. They are the ones who willingly and joyfully give fast offerings to help those of us in need. You are receiving the fruits of their faith and determination to follow Jesus Christ."

My fellow disciples of Christ, let us not underestimate the marvelous work the Lord is doing through *us*, His Church, despite our shortcomings. Sometimes we are givers and sometimes we are receivers, but we are all one family in Christ. His Church is the structure He has given to guide and bless us as we worship Him and serve each other.

Some sisters have apologized to me, thinking they are not active members of Relief Society because they are serving in Primary or Young Women. Those sisters are among the most active members of Relief Society because they are helping our precious children and youth strengthen their faith in Jesus Christ.

Relief Society is not limited to a room in a building, a Sunday lesson, an activity, or a presidency at the local or general level. Relief Society is the covenant women of the Church; it is *us—each of us* and *all of us*. It is our "global community of compassion and service."[12] Anywhere and everywhere we go, we are always part of Relief Society as we strive to fulfill its divine purpose, which is for women to accomplish God's work in individual as well as collective ways[13] by providing relief: "relief of poverty, relief of illness; relief of doubt, relief of ignorance—relief of all that hinders . . . joy and progress."[14]

Similar belonging exists in elders quorums and organizations of the Church for all ages, including our children and youth. The Church is more than the buildings and the ecclesiastical structure; the Church is *us*, the members. *We* are The Church of Jesus Christ of Latter-day Saints, with Christ at the head and the prophet as His mouthpiece. The Lord has said:

"Behold, this is my doctrine—whosoever repenteth and cometh unto me, the same is my church. . . .

"And . . . whosoever is of my church, and endureth of my church to the end, him will I establish upon my rock."[15]

Sisters and brothers, let us realize how privileged we are to belong to the Church of Jesus Christ, where we can unite our faith, hearts, strengths, minds, and hands for Him to perform His mighty miracles. "For the body [of Christ's Church] is not one member, but many."[16]

A teenage boy told his mother, "When I was little, every time I gave one dollar in tithing, I thought that with that *one* dollar a *whole* meetinghouse would be built. Isn't that silly?"

Touched, she replied, "That is lovely! Did you picture them in your mind?"

"Yes!" he exclaimed. "They were beautiful, and there were millions of them!"[17]

My dear friends, let us have the faith of a child and rejoice in knowing that even our smallest efforts are making a significant difference in God's kingdom.

Our purpose in His kingdom should be to bring each other to Christ. As we read in the scriptures, the Savior extended this invitation to the Nephites:

"Have ye any that are sick among you? Bring them hither. Have ye any that are . . . afflicted in any manner? Bring them hither and I will heal them, for I have compassion upon you; my bowels are filled with mercy.

". . . I see that your faith is sufficient that I should heal you."[18]

Do we not all have afflictions that can be brought to the Savior's feet? While some of us have physical challenges, many more battle with emotional strife, others struggle to nurture social connections, and we all seek respite when our spirits are challenged. We are *all* afflicted in some manner.

We read that "all the multitude, with one accord, did go forth with their sick and . . . with *all* them that were afflicted in any manner; and he *did* heal them *every one* as they were brought forth unto him.

"And they did all, both they who had been healed and they who were whole, bow down at his feet, and did worship him."[19]

From a little boy who pays tithing with faith, to a single mother in need of the Lord's empowering grace, to a father struggling to provide for his family, to our ancestors in need of the ordinances of salvation and exaltation, to each of us who renews covenants with God every week, we need each other, and we can bring each other to the Savior's redeeming healing.

My dear sisters and brothers, let us follow Jesus Christ's invitation to bring ourselves and our afflictions to Him. When we come to Him and bring those we love to Him, He sees our faith. He will make them whole, and He will make us whole.

As "the peaceable followers of Christ,"[20] we are striving to become "of one heart and one mind"[21] and to be humble; submissive; gentle; easy to be entreated; full of patience and long-suffering; temperate in all things; diligent in keeping the commandments of God at all times; full of faith, hope, and charity; and abounding in good works.[22] We are striving to become like Jesus Christ.

I testify that as Christ's Church, we are the means through which, as President Russell M. Nelson taught, "our Savior and Redeemer, Jesus Christ, will perform some of His mightiest works between now and when He comes again."[23]

The Lord has said:

"Behold, I will hasten my work in its time.

"And I give unto you . . . a commandment that you assemble yourselves together, and organize yourselves, and prepare yourselves, and sanctify yourselves; yea, purify your hearts, and cleanse your hands and your feet before me, that I may make you clean."[24]

May we respond to this divine invitation and joyfully assemble, organize, prepare, and sanctify ourselves is my humble prayer in the name of Jesus Christ, amen.

Notes

1. John 1:46; see also Dieter F. Uchtdorf, "Missionary Work: Sharing What Is in Your Heart," *Ensign* or *Liahona*, May 2019, 15–18; David A. Bednar, "Come and See," *Ensign* or *Liahona*, Nov. 2014, 107–10.
2. Isaiah 25:4; Doctrine and Covenants 115:6.
3. Moroni 6:4.
4. See Gordon B. Hinckley, "Converts and Young Men," *Ensign*, May 1997, 47–50.
5. See, for example, Matthew 28:19–20; Ephesians 4:11–13; Jacob 5:61–62, 71–72; 3 Nephi 26:20–21; 27:5–8; 28:23; Doctrine and Covenants 20; 21; 88:73–74; 115:4; 138:30–35, 55–56; Moses 5:58–59; 6:22–23; Abraham 3:22–28; 4.
6. Moses 1:39.

7. See, for example, Exodus 25:8; Deuteronomy 12:5–14; Doctrine and Covenants 59:9; 109:8.

8. See Russell M. Nelson, "The Temple and Your Spiritual Foundation," *Liahona*, Nov. 2021, 93–96; David A. Bednar, "With the Power of God in Great Glory," *Liahona*, Nov. 2021, 28–30.

9. Doctrine and Covenants 84:20; see also 1 Nephi 14:14; Doctrine and Covenants 95:8; *General Handbook: Serving in The Church of Jesus Christ of Latter-day Saints*, 3.5, 27.2, ChurchofJesusChrist.org.

10. See Mosiah 18:25; Alma 6:6; 15:18; 4 Nephi 1:12; Moroni 6:4–6; Doctrine and Covenants 20:75; 59:9; 101:22.

11. L. Tom Perry, "The Tradition of Light and Testimony," *Ensign*, Dec. 2012, 30; *Liahona*, Dec. 2012, 12.

12. "The Role of Women," *Muslims and Latter-day Saints: Beliefs, Values, and Lifestyles*, ChurchofJesusChrist.org.

13. See *General Handbook*, 9.1.1.

14. John A. Widtsoe, *Evidences and Reconciliations*, arr. G. Homer Durham, 3 vols. in 1 (1960), 308.

15. Doctrine and Covenants 10:67, 69; see also 1 Corinthians 12:12–31; Mosiah 18:17; 3 Nephi 18:5–16; 26:21.

16. 1 Corinthians 12:14.

17. See Reyna I. Aburto, *Reaching for the Savior* (2021), 89–90.

18. 3 Nephi 17:7–8.

19. 3 Nephi 17:9–10; emphasis added.

20. Moroni 7:3.

21. Moses 7:18.

22. See Alma 7:23–24.

23. Russell M. Nelson, "Revelation for the Church, Revelation for Our Lives," *Ensign* or *Liahona*, May 2018, 96.

24. Doctrine and Covenants 88:73–74.

BUT WE HEEDED THEM NOT _(1 NEPHI 8:33)

ELDER DAVID A. BEDNAR
Of the Quorum of the Twelve Apostles

My wife, Susan, our three sons and their wives, all of our grand-children, and Elder Quentin L. Cook, my seatmate in the Quorum of the Twelve for almost 15 years, all readily will attest to the fact that I do not sing well. But in spite of my lack of vocal talent, I love to sing the hymns of the Restoration. The combination of in-spired lyrics and majestic melodies helps me to learn essential gospel principles and stirs my soul.

One hymn that has blessed my life in remarkable ways is "Let Us All Press On." Recently I have been pondering and learning about a specific phrase in the refrain of that hymn. "*We will heed not what the wicked may say, but the Lord alone we will obey.*"[1]

We will heed not.

As I sing "Let Us All Press On," I often think of the people in Lehi's vision pressing forward on the path that led to the tree of life who were not merely "clinging to"[2] but were "continually holding fast to the rod of iron, until they came forth and fell down and partook of the fruit of the tree."[3] Lehi described multitudes in the great and spacious building that were pointing "the finger of scorn at [him] and those . . . partaking of the fruit."[4] His response to the jeers and insults is magnificent and memorable: "*But we heeded them not.*"[5]

I pray that the Holy Ghost will bless and enlighten each of us as we consider together how we can be strengthened to "heed not" the evil influences and mocking voices of the contemporary world in which we live.

Heed Not

The word *heed* suggests taking notice of or paying attention to someone or something. Thus, the lyrics of the hymn "Let Us All Press On" admonish us to make an affirmative decision to pay no attention to "what the wicked may say." And Lehi and the people with him who were partaking of the fruit of the tree provide a strong example of not paying attention to the mocking and scorn that so frequently come from the great and spacious building.

The doctrine of Christ written "with the Spirit of the living God . . . in fleshy tables of [our hearts]"[6] increases our capacity to "heed not" the many distractions, taunts, and diversions in our fallen world. For example, faith focused in and on the Lord Jesus Christ fortifies us with spiritual strength. Faith in the Redeemer is a principle of action and of power. As we act in accordance with the truths of His gospel, we are blessed with the spiritual capacity to press forward through the challenges of mortality while focusing on the joys the Savior offers to us. Truly, "if we do what's right we have no need to fear, for the Lord, our helper, will ever be near."[7]

A Personal Connection through Covenants

Entering into sacred covenants and worthily receiving priesthood ordinances yoke us with and bind us to the Lord Jesus Christ and Heavenly Father.[8] This simply means that we trust in the Savior as our Advocate[9] and Mediator[10] and rely on His merits, mercy, and grace[11] during the journey of life. As we are steadfast in coming unto Christ and are yoked with Him, we receive the cleansing, healing, and strengthening blessings of His infinite and eternal Atonement.[12]

Living and loving covenant commitments creates a connection with the Lord that is deeply personal and spiritually powerful. As we honor the conditions of sacred covenants and ordinances, we gradually and incrementally are drawn closer to Him[13] and experience the impact of His divinity and living reality in our lives. Jesus then becomes much more than the central character in scripture stories; His example and teachings influence our every desire, thought, and action.

I frankly do not have the ability to describe adequately the precise nature and power of our covenant connection with the resurrected and living Son of God. But I witness that the connections with Him and Heavenly Father are real and are the ultimate sources of assurance, peace, joy, and the spiritual strength that enable us to "fear not, though the enemy deride."[14] As covenant-making and covenant-keeping disciples of Jesus Christ, we can be blessed to take "courage, for the Lord is on our side"[15] and pay no attention to evil influences and secular scoffing.

As I visit with members of the Church around the world, I often ask them this question: what helps you to "heed not" worldly influences, mocking, and scorn? Their answers are most instructive.

Valiant members often highlight the importance of inviting the power of the Holy Ghost into their lives through meaningful scripture study, fervent prayer, and proper preparation to participate in the ordinance of the sacrament. Also mentioned frequently are the spiritual support of faithful family members and trusted friends, the vital lessons learned through ministering and serving in the Lord's restored Church, and the capacity to discern the absolute emptiness of anything in or coming from the great and spacious building.

I have noted in these member responses a particular pattern that is especially significant. First and foremost, these disciples have firm testimonies of Heavenly Father's plan of happiness and the role of Jesus Christ as our Redeemer and Savior. And second, their spiritual knowledge and conviction are individual, personal, and specific; they are not general and abstract. I listen to these devoted souls speak of covenants providing strength to overcome opposition and their connection with the living Lord supporting them through times both good and bad. To these individuals, Jesus Christ indeed is a personal Savior.

Gospel covenants and ordinances operate in our lives much like a compass. A compass is a device used to indicate the cardinal directions of north, south, east, and west for purposes of navigation and geographic orientation. In a similar way, our covenants and ordinances point us to and help us always remember our connection with the Lord Jesus Christ as we progress along the covenant path.

The cardinal direction for all of us in mortality is to come unto and be perfected in Christ.[16] Holy covenants and ordinances help us to keep our focus upon the Savior and strive, with His grace,[17] to become more like Him. Most assuredly, "an unseen [power] will aid me and you in the glorious cause of truth."[18]

Holding Fast to the Iron Rod

Our covenant connection with God and Jesus Christ is the channel through which we can receive the capacity and strength to "heed not." And this bond is strengthened as we continually hold fast to the rod of iron. But as Nephi's brethren asked, "What meaneth the rod of iron which our father saw . . . ?

"And [Nephi] said unto them that it was the *word of God*; and whoso would hearken unto *the word of God*, and would *hold fast unto it*, they would never perish; neither could the temptations and the fiery darts of the adversary overpower them unto blindness, to lead them away to destruction."[19]

Please note that the ability to resist the temptations and the fiery darts of the adversary is promised to those individuals who "hold fast to" rather than merely "cling to" the word of God.

Interestingly, the Apostle John described Jesus Christ as the Word.[20]

"In the beginning was *the Word*, and *the Word* was with God, and *the Word* was God. . . .

"All things were made by him; and without him was not any thing made that was made. . . .

"And *the Word* was made flesh, and dwelt among us, (and we beheld his glory, the glory as of the only begotten of the Father,) full of grace and truth."[21]

Therefore, one of the names of Jesus Christ is "The Word."[22]

In addition, the eighth article of faith states, "We believe the Bible to be *the word of God* as far as it is translated correctly; we also believe the Book of Mormon to be *the word of God*."[23]

Thus, the teachings of the Savior, as recorded in the holy scriptures, also are "the word."

Let me suggest that holding fast to the word of God entails (1) remembering, honoring, and strengthening the personal connection we have with the Savior and His Father through the covenants and ordinances of the restored gospel and (2) prayerfully, earnestly, and consistently using the holy scriptures and the teachings of living prophets and apostles as sure sources of revealed truth. As we are bound and "hold fast" to the Lord and are transformed by living His doctrine,[24] I promise that individually and collectively we will be blessed to "stand in holy places, and shall not be moved."[25] If we abide in Christ, then He will abide in and walk with us.[26] Surely, "in the days of trial his Saints he will cheer, and prosper the cause of truth."[27]

Testimony

Press on. Hold fast. Heed not.

I witness that fidelity to the covenants and ordinances of the Savior's restored gospel enables us to *press on* in the work of the Lord, to *hold fast* to Him as the Word of God, and to *heed not* the allurements of the adversary. In the fight for right, may each of us wield a sword, even "the mighty sword of truth,"[28] in the sacred name of the Lord Jesus Christ, amen.

Notes

1. "Let Us All Press On," *Hymns*, no. 243; emphasis added.
2. 1 Nephi 8:24.
3. 1 Nephi 8:30.
4. 1 Nephi 8:33.
5. 1 Nephi 8:33; emphasis added.
6. 2 Corinthians 3:3.
7. *Hymns*, no. 243.
8. See Matthew 11:28–30.
9. See Moroni 7:28; Doctrine and Covenants 110:4.
10. See John 14:6; 1 Timothy 2:5; Doctrine and Covenants 107:19.
11. See 2 Nephi 2:8.
12. See Alma 7:11–13.
13. See 3 Nephi 27:14–15.
14. *Hymns*, no. 243.
15. *Hymns*, no. 243.
16. See 3 Nephi 12:20; Moroni 10:32–33.
17. See 2 Nephi 25:23.
18. *Hymns*, no. 243.
19. 1 Nephi 15:23–24; emphasis added.
20. Joseph Smith Translation, John 1:1 reads: "In the beginning was the gospel preached through the Son. And the gospel was the word, and the word was with the Son, and the Son was with God, and the Son was of God" (in the Bible appendix).
21. John 1:1, 3, 14; emphasis added.
22. "The Word" is a title of Jesus Christ found in several places in the scriptures (see John 1:1, 14; 1 John 1:1; Revelation 19:13; Doctrine and Covenants 93:8–10; Moses 1:32).

23. Articles of Faith 1:8; emphasis added.
24. See 2 Corinthians 5:17; Mosiah 3:19; 5:2; 27:25–26; Alma 5:49; Moroni 10:32.
25. Doctrine and Covenants 45:32.
26. See John 15:4–8; Doctrine and Covenants 50:41–43; Moses 6:33–34, 39.
27. *Hymns*, no. 243.
28. *Hymns*, no. 243.

FOLLOWING JESUS: BEING A PEACEMAKER

ELDER NEIL L. ANDERSEN
Of the Quorum of the Twelve Apostles

My dear brothers and sisters, as we experience sobering days of commotion, contention, and, for many, deep suffering, our hearts are filled with overwhelming gratitude for our Savior and the eternal blessings of the restored gospel of Jesus Christ. We love Him and we trust Him, and we pray that we will forever follow Him.

The Challenge of Social Media

The powerful impact of the internet is a blessing and a challenge, unique to our time.

In a world of social media and information superhighways, one person's voice can be multiplied exponentially. That voice, whether true or false, whether fair or prejudicial, whether kind or cruel, moves instantly across the world.

Social media posts of thoughtfulness and goodness are often quietly under the radar, while words of contempt and anger are frequently thundering in our ears, whether with political philosophy, people in the news, or opinions on the pandemic. No one or no subject, including the Savior and His restored gospel, is immune from this social phenomenon of polarized voices.

Becoming a Peacemaker

The Sermon on the Mount is a message for all but was specifically given to the Savior's disciples, those who had chosen to follow Him.

The Lord taught how to live, then and now, in a contemptuous world. "Blessed are the peacemakers," He declared, "for they shall be called the children of God."[1]

By the shield of our faith in Jesus Christ, we become peacemakers, quenching—meaning to calm, cool, or extinguish—all the fiery darts of the adversary.[2]

As we do our part, His promise is that we will be called the "children of God." Every person on earth is the "offspring"[3] of God, but to be called the "children of God" means much, much more. As we come unto Jesus Christ and make covenants with Him, we become "his seed" and "heirs of the kingdom,"[4] "children of Christ, his sons, and his daughters."[5]

How does a peacemaker calm and cool the fiery darts? Certainly not by shrinking before those who disparage us. Rather, we remain confident in our faith, sharing our beliefs with conviction but always void of anger or malice.[6]

Recently, after seeing a strongly worded opinion piece that was critical of the Church, Reverend Amos C. Brown, a national civil rights leader and pastor of the Third Baptist Church in San Francisco, responded:

"I respect the experience and perspective of the individual who wrote those words. Granted, I don't see what he sees."

"I count it one of my life's greatest joys to know these leaders [of the Church], including President Russell M. Nelson. They are, in my estimation, the embodiment of the best leadership our country has to offer."

He then added: "We can gripe about the way things were. We can refuse to acknowledge all the good going on now. . . . But these approaches will not heal our national divisions. . . . As Jesus taught, we don't eradicate evil with more evil. We love generously and live mercifully, even toward those we think to be our enemies."[7]

Reverend Brown is a peacemaker. He calmly and respectfully cooled the fiery darts. Peacemakers are not passive; they are persuasive in the Savior's way.[8]

What gives us the inner strength to cool, calm, and quench the fiery darts aimed toward the truths we love? The strength comes from our faith in Jesus Christ and our faith in His words.

"Blessed are ye, when men shall revile you, . . . and shall say all manner of evil against you falsely, for my sake.

". . . For great is your reward in heaven: for so persecuted they the prophets which were before you."[9]

The Importance of Agency

Two important principles guide our desire to be peacemakers.

First, our Heavenly Father has given each individual his or her moral agency, with the ability to choose one's own path.[10] This agency is one of the greatest gifts of God.

Second, with this agency, our Heavenly Father allowed for "opposition in all things."[11] We "taste the bitter, that [we] may know to prize the good."[12] Opposition should not surprise us. We learn to distinguish good from evil.

We rejoice in the blessing of agency, understanding that there will be many who do not believe what we believe. In fact, few in the latter days will choose to make their faith in Jesus Christ central to all they think and do.[13]

Because of social media platforms, one voice of disbelief can appear to be a multitude of negative voices,[14] but even if it is a multitude of voices, we choose the path of peacemakers.

The Lord's Leaders

Some view the First Presidency and the Quorum of the Twelve as having worldly motives, like political, business, and cultural leaders.

However, we come very differently to our responsibilities. We are not elected or selected from applications. Without any specific professional preparation, we are called and ordained to bear testimony of the name of Jesus Christ throughout the world until our final breath. We endeavor to bless the sick, the lonely, the downhearted, and the poor and to strengthen the kingdom of God. We seek to know the Lord's will and to proclaim it, especially to those who seek eternal life.[15]

Although our humble desire is for the Savior's teachings to be honored by all, the words of the Lord through His prophets are often contrary to the thinking and trends of the world. It has always been so.[16]

The Savior said to His Apostles:

"If the world [hates] you, ye know that it hated me before it hated you. . . .

". . . All these things will they do . . . because *they know not him* that sent me."[17]

Caring for All

We genuinely love and care for all our neighbors, whether or not they believe as we do. Jesus taught us in the parable of the Good Samaritan that those of different beliefs should sincerely reach out to help anyone in need, being peacemakers, pursuing good and noble causes.

In February, a headline in the *Arizona Republic* stated, "Bipartisan bill supported by Latter-day Saints would protect gay and transgender Arizonans."[18]

We, as Latter-day Saints, are "pleased to be part of a coalition of faith, business, LGBTQ people and community leaders who have worked together in a spirit of trust and mutual respect."[19]

President Russell M. Nelson once thoughtfully asked, "Cannot boundary lines exist without becoming battle lines?"[20]

We endeavor to be "peaceable followers of Christ."[21]

The Times Not to Respond

Some of the attacks upon the Savior were so malicious that He said nothing. "And the chief priests and scribes . . . vehemently accused him . . . and mocked him," but Jesus "answered [them] nothing."[22] There are times when being a peacemaker means that we resist the impulse to respond and instead, with dignity, remain quiet.[23]

It is heartbreaking for all of us when harsh or dismissive words about the Savior, His followers, and His Church are spoken or published by those who once stood with us, took the sacrament with us, and testified with us of the divine mission of Jesus Christ.[24]

This also happened during the Savior's ministry.

Some of the disciples of Jesus who were with Him during His most majestic miracles determined to "[walk] no more with him."[25]

Sadly, not all will remain firm in their love for the Savior and their determination to keep His commandments.[26]

Jesus taught us to withdraw from the circle of anger and contention. In one example, after the Pharisees confronted Jesus and counseled how they might destroy Him, the scriptures say that Jesus withdrew Himself from them,[27] and miracles occurred as "great multitudes followed him, and he healed them all."[28]

Blessing the Lives of Others

We too can move away from contention and bless the lives of others[29] while not isolating ourselves in our own corner.

In Mbuji-Mayi, Democratic Republic of the Congo, initially some were critical of the Church, not understanding our beliefs or knowing our members.

Some time ago, Kathy and I attended a very special Church service in Mbuji-Mayi. The children were dressed immaculately, with bright eyes and big smiles. I had hoped to speak to them about their education but learned that many were not attending school. Our leaders, with very nominal humanitarian funds, found a way to help.[30] Now, more than 400 students—girls and boys, members as well as those not of our faith—are welcomed and taught by 16 teachers who are members of the Church of Jesus Christ.

Fourteen-year-old Kalanga Muya said, "[Having little money,] I spent four years without attending school. . . . I am so grateful for what the Church has done. . . . I can now read, write, and speak French."[31] Speaking of this initiative, the mayor of Mbuji-Mayi said, "I am inspired by The Church of Jesus Christ of Latter-day Saints because while [other] churches are being divided each one in his corner . . . [you are working] with [others] to help the community in need."[32]

Love One Another

Each time I read John chapter 13, I am reminded of the Savior's perfect example as a peacemaker. Jesus lovingly washed the feet of the Apostles. Then, we read, "he was troubled in spirit"[33] as He thought about one He loved preparing to betray Him. I have tried to imagine the thoughts and feelings of the Savior as Judas left. Interestingly, at that sobering moment, Jesus spoke no more about His "troubling" feelings or about betrayal. Rather, He spoke to His Apostles about love, His words cascading through the centuries:

"A new commandment I give unto you, That ye love one another; as I have loved you. . . .

"By this shall all men know that ye are my disciples, if ye have love one to another."[34]

May we love Him and love one another. May we be peacemakers, that we may be called the "children of God," I pray in the name of Jesus Christ, amen.

Notes

1. Matthew 5:9.
2. See Ephesians 6:16; Doctrine and Covenants 3:8.
3. Acts 17:28.
4. Mosiah 15:11.
5. Mosiah 5:7.
6. President Dallin H. Oaks said: "Followers of Christ should be examples of civility. We should love all people, be good listeners, and show concern for their sincere beliefs. Though we may disagree, we should not be disagreeable. Our stands and communications on controversial topics should not be contentious" ("Loving Others and Living with Differences," *Ensign* or *Liahona*, Nov. 2014, 27).
7. "Amos C. Brown: Follow the LDS Church's Example to Heal Divisions and Move Forward," *Salt Lake Tribune*, Jan. 20, 2022, sltrib.com.
8. Elder Dale G. Renlund said, "When love of Christ envelops our lives, we approach disagreements with meekness, patience, and kindness" ("The Peace of Christ Abolishes Enmity," *Liahona*, Nov. 2021, 84).
9. Matthew 5:11–12.
10. See 2 Nephi 10:23.
11. 2 Nephi 2:11.
12. Moses 6:55.
13. See 1 Nephi 14:12.
14. Recent data shows that as many as 3 out of 5 people share a headline for a story they have not even read (see Caitlin Dewey, "6 in 10 of You Will Share This Link without Reading It, a New, Depressing Study Says," *Washington Post*, June 16, 2015, washingtonpost.com; Maksym Gabielkov and others, "Social Clicks: What and Who Gets Read on Twitter?" [paper presented at the 2016 ACM Sigmetrics International Conference on Measurement and Modeling of Computer Science, June 14, 2016], dl.acm.org).
15. Don't be surprised if at times your personal views are not initially in harmony with the teachings of the Lord's prophet. These are moments of learning, of humility, when we go to our knees in prayer. We walk forward in faith, trusting in God, knowing that with time we will receive more spiritual clarity from our Heavenly Father.
16. See Doctrine and Covenants 1:14–16.
17. John 15:18, 21; emphasis added.
18. "Bipartisan Bill Supported by Latter-day Saints Would Protect Gay and Transgender Arizonans," *Arizona Republic*, Feb. 7, 2022, azcentral.com.

19. "Why the Church of Jesus Christ Supports a New Bipartisan Religious Freedom and Non-discrimination Bill in Arizona," Feb. 7, 2022, newsroom.ChurchofJesusChrist.org.

20. Russell M. Nelson, "Teach Us Tolerance and Love," *Ensign*, May 1994, 69.

21. Moroni 7:3. President Gordon B. Hinckley said: "We must not only be tolerant, but we must cultivate a spirit of affirmative gratitude for those who do not see things quite as we see them. We do not in any way have to compromise our theology, our convictions, our knowledge of eternal truth as it has been revealed by the God of Heaven. We can offer our own witness of the truth, quietly, sincerely, honestly, but never in a manner that will give offense to others. . . . We must learn to accord appreciation and respect for others who are as sincere in their beliefs and practices as are we" ("Out of Your Experience Here" [Brigham Young University devotional, Oct. 16, 1990], 6, speeches.byu.edu).

22. See Luke 23:9–11.

23. Elder Dieter F. Uchtdorf said: "As followers of Jesus Christ, we follow [His] example. We do not shame or attack others. We seek to love God and serve our neighbors. We seek to joyfully keep God's commandments and live by gospel principles" ("Five Messages That All of God's Children Need to Hear" [Brigham Young University Education Week devotional, Aug. 17, 2021], 5, speeches.byu.edu).

24. Elder Neal A. Maxwell said: "Church members will live in this wheat-and-tares situation until the Millennium. Some real tares even masquerade as wheat, including the few eager individuals who lecture the rest of us about Church doctrines in which they no longer believe. They criticize the use of Church resources to which they no longer contribute. They condescendingly seek to counsel the Brethren whom they no longer sustain. Confrontive, except of themselves, of course, they leave the Church, but they cannot leave the Church alone" ("Becometh As a Child," *Ensign*, May 1996, 68).

25. John 6:66.

26. "The pleasures of sin [are only] for a season" (see Hebrews 11:24–26).

27. See Matthew 12:1–15.

28. Matthew 12:15.

29. See 3 Nephi 11:29–30.

30. With the help of the Don Bosco Foundation, the school program received valuable expertise in teaching and materials.

31. Muleka, a parent, said: "I love this program because it has provided my daughter . . . the chance to . . . learn to read and write and hope for a better future. I could not send her to school because I am just selling corn flour in the market earning . . . enough only for food. I greatly thank the Church for this." Sister Monique, a teacher, said: "This program came as a great blessing for these children. In my class . . . most of them are orphans. They are loving it, regularly attending classes and doing their homework" (comments and photos supplied by Elder Joseph W. Sitati, Feb. 24, 2022).

32. Mayor Louis d'Or Ntumba Tshiapota, remarks in a public meeting concerning the Mbuji-Mayi literacy project initiated by The Church of Jesus Christ of Latter-day Saints, Oct. 10, 2021.

33. John 13:21.

34. John 13:34–35.

A MIGHTY CHANGE OF HEART:
"I HAVE NOTHING MORE TO GIVE YOU"

ELDER EDUARDO GAVARRET
Of the Seventy

Introduction

On Friday, October 28, 1588, having lost its rudder to being governed solely by oar, the ship *La Girona*, belonging to the great Spanish Armada, collided with the rocks of Lacada Point in Northern Ireland.[1]

The ship capsized. One of the castaways struggling to survive wore a gold ring given to him a few months earlier by his wife with the inscription, "I have nothing more to give you."[2]

"I have nothing more to give you"—a phrase and a ring with the design of a hand holding a heart, an expression of love from a wife to her husband.

Scripture Connection

When I read this story, it made a deep impression on me, and I thought of the request made by the Savior: "And ye shall offer for a sacrifice unto me a broken heart and a contrite spirit."[3]

I also thought of the people's reaction to King Benjamin's words: "Yea, we believe all the words which thou hast spoken unto us . . . , which has wrought a mighty change in us, or in our hearts, that we have no more disposition to do evil, but to do good continually."[4]

Personal Connection

Let me share with you an experience I had when I was 12 years old, the effect of which lasts to this day.

My mother said, "Eduardo, hurry up. We are late for the Church meetings."

"Mom, I'm going to stay with Dad today," I replied.

"Are you sure? You have to attend your priesthood quorum meeting," she said.

I replied, "Poor Dad! He is going to be left alone. I'm going to stay with him today."

Dad was not a member of The Church of Jesus Christ of Latter-day Saints.

My mother and sisters went to Sunday meetings. So I went to meet Dad in his workshop, where he liked to be on Sundays, and as I had told my mother, I spent a while, that is, a few minutes with him, and then I asked, "Dad, is everything all right?"

He kept up his hobby of repairing radios and clocks, and he just smiled at me.

Then I told him, "I'm going to go play with my friends."

Dad, without looking up, said to me, "Today is Sunday. Aren't you supposed to go to church?"

"Yes, but today I told Mom I wouldn't go," I replied. Dad went on about his business, and for me, that was permission to leave.

That morning there was an important soccer game, and my friends had told me that I couldn't miss it because we had to win that game.

My challenge was that I had to pass in front of the chapel to get to the soccer field.

Determined, I dashed towards the soccer field and stopped before the great stumbling block, the chapel. I ran to the opposite sidewalk, where there were some big trees, and I decided to run between them so that no one would see me since it was the time the members were arriving at the meetings.

I arrived just in time for the start of the game. I was able to play and go home before my mother got home.

Everything had gone well; our team had won, and I was thrilled. But that well-executed run onto the field did not go unnoticed by the deacons quorum adviser.

Brother Félix Espinoza had seen me running quickly from tree to tree, trying not to be discovered.

At the beginning of the week, Brother Espinoza came to my house and asked to speak with me. He didn't say anything about what he had seen on Sunday, nor did he ask me why I had missed my meeting.

He just handed me a manual and said, "I would like you to teach the priesthood class on Sunday. I have marked the lesson for you. It is not so difficult. I want you to read it, and I will come by in two days to help you with the preparation for the lesson." Having said this, he handed me the manual and left.

I didn't want to teach the class, but I couldn't bring myself to tell him no. I had planned that Sunday to stay with my father again—meaning, there was another important soccer game.

Brother Espinoza was a person whom young people admired.[5] He had found the restored gospel and changed his life or, in other words, his heart.

When Saturday afternoon arrived, I thought, "Well, maybe tomorrow I'll wake up sick, and I won't have to go to church." It wasn't the soccer game that worried me anymore; it was the class I had to teach, especially a lesson about the Sabbath day.

Sunday came, and I woke up healthier than ever. I had no excuse—no escape.

It was the first time I would teach a lesson, but Brother Espinoza was there by my side, and that was the day of a mighty change of heart for me.

From that moment on, I began to keep the Sabbath day holy, and over time, in the words of President Russell M. Nelson, the Sabbath day has become a delight.[6]

"Lord, I give You everything; I have nothing more to give You."

Obtaining

How do we obtain that mighty change of heart? It is initiated and eventually occurs

1. when we study the scriptures to obtain the knowledge that will strengthen our faith in Jesus Christ, which will create a desire to change;[7]
2. when we cultivate that desire through prayer and fasting;[8]
3. when we act, according to the word studied or received,

and we make a covenant to surrender our hearts to Him, just as with King Benjamin's people.[9]

Recognition and Covenant

How do we know that our heart is changing?[10]

1. When we want to please God in all things.[11]
2. When we treat others with love, respect, and consideration.[12]
3. When we see that the attributes of Christ are becoming part of our character.[13]
4. When we feel the guidance of the Holy Spirit more constantly.[14]
5. When we keep a commandment that has been difficult for us to obey and then continue to live it.[15]

When we listen carefully to our leaders' advice and cheerfully decide to follow it, have we not experienced a mighty change of heart?

"Lord, I give You everything; I have nothing more to give You."

Maintenance and Benefits

How do we maintain the mighty change?

1. When we partake of the sacrament weekly and renew the covenant to take upon us the name of Christ, always remember Him, and keep His commandments.[16]
2. When we turn our lives toward the temple.[17] Regular temple attendance will help us maintain a new and renewed heart as we participate in the ordinances.
3. When we love and serve our neighbors by ministering activities and missionary work.[18]

Then for our great joy, that inner change is strengthened and spreads until it abounds in good works.[19]

This mighty change of heart brings us a feeling of freedom, trust, and peace.[20]

This change of heart is not an event; it takes faith, repentance, and constant spiritual work to happen. It begins when we desire to submit our will to the Lord, and it materializes when we enter into and keep covenants with Him.

That individual action has a positive effect both on us and on the people around us.

In the words of President Russell M. Nelson, "Imagine how quickly the devastating conflicts throughout the world—and those in our individual lives—would be resolved if we all chose to follow Jesus Christ and heed His teachings."[21] This action of following the Savior's teachings leads to a mighty change of heart.

Dear brothers and sisters, young people, and children, as we participate in the conference this weekend, let the words of our prophets, which will come from the Lord, enter our hearts to experience a mighty change.

For those who have not yet joined the Lord's restored Church, I invite you to listen to the missionaries with a sincere desire to know what God expects of you and experience that inner transformation.[22]

Today is the day to decide to follow the Lord Jesus Christ. "Lord, I give You my heart; I have nothing more to give You."

Just as the ring was recovered from that shipwreck, when we give our hearts to God, we are rescued from the raging seas of this life, and in the process we are refined and purified through the Atonement of Christ and become "children of Christ," being spiritually "born of Him."[23] Of this I testify in the name of Jesus Christ, amen.

Notes

1. See Pedro Luis Chinchilla, "*La Girona*: La Historia del Mayor Naufragio de la Gran Armada," armadainvencible.org/la-girona.
2. Ring in Ulster Museum, Belfast, Northern Ireland.
3. 3 Nephi 9:20.
4. Mosiah 5:2.
5. Félix Espinoza was a national champion of Basque *pelota*. He participated in local and worldwide championships. He passed away on March 5, 2022.
6. See Russell M. Nelson, "The Sabbath Is a Delight," *Ensign* or *Liahona*, May 2015, 129–32.
7. See 2 Timothy 3:15–17.
8. See Alma 17:3.
9. See Mosiah 5:5.
10. See Mosiah 5:2–5; Alma 5:26–29.
11. See John 8:29.
12. See Leviticus 19:18; Matthew 22:39.

13. See *Preach My Gospel: A Guide to Missionary Service* (2019), chapter 6, "How Do I Develop Christlike Attributes?," 121–32.
14. See Doctrine and Covenants 11:12–13.
15. See Proverbs 4:4; 1 Timothy 1:5.
16. See Doctrine and Covenants 20:77–79.
17. See Mosiah 2:6.
18. See Mosiah 2:17; Doctrine and Covenants 81:5.
19. See Ether 12:4.
20. See 4 Nephi 1:15–16.
21. Russell M. Nelson, "Pure Truth, Pure Doctrine, Pure Revelation," *Liahona*, Nov. 2021, 6.
22. See Jeremiah 29:12–13; Mosiah 18:10; Doctrine and Covenants 20:37.
23. Mosiah 5:7.

LADDER OF FAITH

ELDER LARRY S. KACHER
Of the Seventy

How will life's challenges affect our faith in Jesus Christ? And what effect will our faith have on the joy and peace we experience in this life?

The year was 1977. The phone rang, and the message tore our hearts apart. Carolyn and Doug Tebbs were in the process of moving to their new home after completing graduate school. The elders quorum had come to load the moving van. Doug, making sure the path was clear before backing out, took one last look. What he could not see was his little daughter, Jennie, dart behind the truck at just the wrong moment. In an instant, their beloved Jennie was gone.

What would happen next? Would the pain they so deeply felt and the inconceivable sense of loss create an irreconcilable chasm between Carolyn and Doug, or would it somehow bind their hearts together and solidify their faith in Heavenly Father's plan?

The road through their afflictions has been long and painful, but from somewhere came the spiritual reserves to not lose hope but to "hold on [their] way."[1] Somehow this incredible couple became even more Christlike. More committed. More compassionate. They believed that, in His time, God would consecrate their afflictions for their gain.[2]

Though the pain and loss would not and could not leave completely, Carolyn and Doug have been comforted by the assurance that by their staying firmly on the covenant path, their beloved Jennie would be theirs forever.[3]

Their example has strengthened my faith in the Lord's plan. We don't see all things. He does. The Lord told Joseph Smith in Liberty Jail that "all these things shall give thee experience, and shall be for thy good. The Son of Man hath descended below them all. Art thou greater than he?"[4]

As we accept the Lord's will, He teaches us how to walk with Him.[5] As a young missionary serving in Tahiti, I was asked to administer to a sick infant. We laid our hands on his head and blessed him to get better. His health began to improve, but then he fell sick again. A second time we blessed him but with the same result. A third request came. We pleaded with the Lord that His will be done. Shortly after, this little spirit returned to his heavenly home.

But we were at peace. We wanted the infant to live, but the Lord had other plans. Accepting His will in place of our own is key to finding joy no matter our circumstances.

The simple faith we have in Jesus Christ as we first begin to learn about Him can remain in our hearts as we confront life's challenges. Our faith in Him can and will guide us through the complexities of life. Indeed, we will find that there is simplicity on the other side of life's complexities[6] as we remain "[steadfast] in Christ, having a perfect brightness of hope."[7]

Part of life's purpose is to allow these potential stumbling blocks to become stepping-stones as we climb what I call the "ladder of faith"—a ladder because it suggests that faith is not static. It can go up or down according to the choices we make.

As we strive to build faith in the Savior, we may not fully comprehend God's love for us, and we may obey His laws out of a sense of obligation. Guilt may even become our primary motivator rather than love. A real connection to Him may not yet have been experienced.

As we seek to increase our faith, we may be confused by what James taught. He reminded us that "faith without works is dead."[8] We may stumble if we think everything depends on us. An overdependence on ourselves can impede our ability to access the powers of heaven.

But as we move toward true faith in Jesus Christ, our mindset begins to change. We recognize that obedience and faith in the Savior qualify us to have His Spirit always to be with us.[9] Obedience is no longer an irritant but becomes a quest.[10] We recognize that obedience to God's commands enables us to be trusted of Him.

With His trust comes increased light. This light guides our journey and allows us to see more clearly the path we should take.

But there is more. As our faith in the Savior increases, we observe a subtle shift that includes a divine understanding of our relationship with God—a steady movement away from "What do I want?" to "What does God want?" Like the Savior, we want to act "not as I will, but as thou wilt."[11] We want to do God's work and be an instrument in His hands.[12]

Our progression is an eternal one. President Russell M. Nelson has taught that there is so much more that Heavenly Father wants us to know.[13] As we progress, we better understand what the Lord taught Joseph Smith: "For if you keep my commandments you shall receive of his fulness, and be glorified in me; . . . I say unto you, you shall receive grace for grace."[14]

How high we climb on the ladder of faith is our decision. Elder Neil L. Andersen taught that "faith is not by chance, but by choice."[15] We can choose to make the choices needed to increase our faith in the Savior.

Consider the impact of the choices made when Laman and Lemuel descended the ladder of faith while Nephi climbed higher. Is there a clearer representation than the difference between Nephi's response of "I will go and do"[16] versus Laman and Lemuel, having just seen an angel, responding with "How is it possible that the Lord will deliver?"[17]

Unbelief blocks our ability to see miracles, whereas a mindset of faith in the Savior unlocks the powers of heaven.

Even when our faith is weak, the Lord's hand will always be stretched out.[18] Years ago I received the assignment to reorganize a stake in Nigeria. At the last minute, there was a change in the date. There was a man in the stake who had decided to skip town for the first conference date. He did not want to risk being called as the stake president.

While he was away, he was in a terrible accident, but he was unharmed. This caused him to consider why his life had been spared. He revisited the decision he had made. He repented and humbly attended the new conference date. And yes, he was called to be the new stake president.

Elder Neal A. Maxwell taught: "Only by aligning our wills with God's is full happiness to be found. Anything less results in a lesser portion."[19]

After doing "all things that lie in our power," then it is time to "stand still . . . to see the salvation of God."[20] I saw this while serving as a ministering brother to the McCormick family. Married for 21 years, Mary Kay served faithfully in her callings. Ken was not a member of the Church and had no interest in becoming one, but loving his wife, he chose to attend church with her.

One Sunday I felt impressed to share my testimony with Ken. I asked him if I could do so. His response was simple and clear: "No, thank you."

I was puzzled. I had felt a prompting and tried to follow it. It was tempting to decide that I had done my part. But after prayer and reflection, I could see that though my intentions were correct, I had relied too much on myself and too little on the Lord.

Later I returned but with a different mindset. I would go simply as an instrument in the Lord's hands, with no other desire than to follow the Spirit. Together with my faithful companion, Gerald Cardon, we entered the McCormick home.

Soon after, I felt prompted to invite Gerald to sing "I Know That My Redeemer Lives."[21] He gave me a questioning look, but having faith in my faith, he did it. A beautiful spirit filled the room. The prompting came to invite Mary Kay and Kristin, their daughter, to share their testimonies. As they did so, the Spirit grew stronger. In fact, after Kristin's testimony, tears were streaming down Ken's cheeks.[22]

God had taken over. Hearts were not just touched but changed forever. Twenty-one years of unbelief were washed away by the power of the Holy Ghost. A week later, Ken was baptized. A year later, Ken and Mary Kay were sealed in the house of the Lord for time and for all eternity.

Together we had experienced what it meant to replace our will with the Lord's will, and our faith in Him increased.

Please consider a few questions posed by God's prophets as you strive to climb your ladder of faith:

Am I stripped of pride?[23]

Do I give place in my heart for the word of God?[24]

Do I allow my afflictions to be consecrated for my gain?[25]

Am I willing to let my will be swallowed up in the will of the Father?[26]

If I have felt to sing the song of redeeming love, can I feel so now?[27]

Do I let God prevail in my life?[28]

If you find your current path in conflict with your faith in the Savior, then please find your way back to Him. Your exaltation and that of your posterity depend on it.

May we plant the seeds of faith deep in our hearts. May we nourish these seeds as we bind ourselves to the Savior by honoring the covenants we have made with Him. In the name of Jesus Christ, amen.

Notes

1. Doctrine and Covenants 122:9.
2. See 2 Nephi 2:2.
3. See Alma 7:11–12.
4. Doctrine and Covenants 122:7–8.
5. See Moses 6:34.
6. See Bruce C. and Marie K. Hafen, "Faith Is Not Blind" (Brigham Young University–Hawaii devotional, Jan. 24, 2017), speeches.byuh.edu.
7. 2 Nephi 31:20.
8. James 2:20.
9. See Moroni 4:3.
10. See Mary Ellen Smoot, "We Are Instruments in the Hands of God," *Ensign*, Nov. 2000, 91; *Liahona*, Jan. 2001, 105.
11. Matthew 26:39.
12. See Alma 29:9.
13. See Russell M. Nelson, "Revelation for the Church, Revelation for Our Lives," *Ensign* or *Liahona*, May 2018, 95.
14. Doctrine and Covenants 93:20.
15. Neil L. Andersen, "Faith Is Not by Chance, but by Choice," *Ensign* or *Liahona*, Nov. 2015, 65.
16. 1 Nephi 3:7.
17. 1 Nephi 3:31.
18. See 3 Nephi 9:14.
19. Neal A. Maxwell, "Swallowed Up in the Will of the Father," *Ensign*, Nov. 1995, 23.
20. Doctrine and Covenants 123:17.

21. "I Know That My Redeemer Lives," *Hymns,* no. 136.
22. See Moroni 6:9.
23. See Alma 5:28.
24. See Alma 32:27–28.
25. See 2 Nephi 2:2.
26. See Mosiah 15:7.
27. See Alma 5:26.
28. See Russell M. Nelson, "Let God Prevail," *Ensign* or *Liahona,* Nov. 2020, 94.

STEADY IN THE STORMS

PRESIDENT HENRY B. EYRING
Second Counselor in the First Presidency

My dear brothers and sisters, we have been blessed today to hear inspired servants of God give counsel and encouragement. Each of us, wherever we are, knows that we live in increasingly perilous times. My prayer is that I might help you stand steady in the storms we face, with a peaceful heart.[1]

The place to begin is to remember that we are each a beloved child of God and that He has inspired servants. Those servants of God have foreseen the times in which we live. The Apostle Paul wrote to Timothy, "This know also, that in the last days perilous times shall come."[2]

Anyone with eyes to see the signs of the times and ears to hear the words of prophets knows that is true. The perils of greatest danger come to us from the forces of wickedness. Those forces are increasing. And so it will become more difficult, not easier, to honor the covenants we must make and keep to live the gospel of Jesus Christ.

For those of us who are concerned for ourselves and for those we love, there is hope in the promise God has made of a place of safety in the storms ahead.

Here is a word picture of that place. It has been repeatedly described by living prophets. For example, as recorded in the Book of Mormon, an inspired and loving father told his sons how to strengthen themselves to stand steady in the storms ahead of them: "And now, my sons, remember, remember that it is upon the rock of our Redeemer, who is Christ, the Son of God, that ye must build your foundation; that when the devil shall send forth his mighty winds, yea, his shafts in the whirlwind, yea, when all his hail and his mighty storm shall beat upon you, it shall have no power over you to drag you down to the gulf of misery and endless wo, because of the rock upon which ye are built, which is a sure foundation, . . . whereon if men build they cannot fall."[3]

The misery and endless woe of which he spoke are the terrible effects of sins should we not fully repent of them. The growing storms are the temptations and the increasing attacks of Satan. It has never been more important than it is now to understand how to build on that sure foundation. For me, there is no better place to look than in the last sermon of King Benjamin, also recorded in the Book of Mormon.

King Benjamin's prophetic words are applicable to us in our day. He knew from his own experience the terrors of war. He had defended his people in combat, relying on the power of God. He saw clearly the terrible powers of Lucifer to tempt, to try to overcome, and to discourage God's children.

He invited his people and us to build on the only sure rock of safety, who is the Savior. He made clear that we are free to choose between right and wrong and that we cannot avoid the consequences of our choices. He spoke directly and sharply because he knew what sorrow would come to those who might not hear and heed his warnings.

Here is how he described the consequences that follow our choice either to follow the prompting of the Spirit or to follow the evil messages that come from Satan, whose intent is to tempt and destroy us:

"For behold, there is a wo pronounced upon him who listeth to obey that [evil] spirit; for if he listeth to obey him, and remaineth and dieth in his sins, the same drinketh damnation to his own soul; for he receiveth for his wages an everlasting punishment, having transgressed the law of God contrary to his own knowledge. . . .

"Therefore if that man repenteth not, and remaineth and dieth an enemy to God, the demands of divine justice do awaken his immortal soul to a lively sense of his own guilt, which doth cause him to shrink from the presence of the Lord, and doth fill his breast with guilt, and pain, and anguish, which is like an unquenchable fire, whose flame ascendeth up forever and ever."

King Benjamin went on to say, "O, all ye old men, and also ye young men, and you little children who can understand my words, for I have spoken plainly unto you that ye might understand, I pray that ye should awake to a remembrance of the awful situation of those that have fallen into transgression."[4]

For me, the power of that warning to repent forms in my mind a picture of the sure time when you and I will stand before the Savior after this life. We want with all our hearts not to shrink but rather to look up at Him, see Him smile, and hear Him say, "Well done, thou good and faithful servant: . . . enter [in]."[5]

King Benjamin makes it clear how we can receive the hope to hear those words if we find the way in this life to have our natures changed through the Atonement of Jesus Christ. That is the only way we can build on the sure foundation and so stand firm during the storms of temptations and trials ahead. King Benjamin describes that change in our natures with a beautiful metaphor that has always touched my heart. It was used by prophets for millennia and by the Lord Himself. It is this: we must become as a child—a little child.

For some, that will not be easy to accept. Most of us want to be strong. We may well see being like a child as being weak. Most parents look for the day when their children act less childish. But King Benjamin, who understood as well as any mortal what it meant to be a man of strength and courage, makes it clear that to be like a child is not to be childish. It is to be like the Savior, who prayed to His Father for strength to be able to do His Father's will and atone for the sins of all of His Father's children and then did it. Our natures must be changed to become as a child to gain the strength we must have to stand steady and at peace in times of peril.

Here is King Benjamin's stirring description of how that change comes: "For the natural man is an enemy to God, and has been from the fall of Adam, and will be, forever and ever, unless he yields to the enticings of the Holy Spirit, and putteth off the natural man and becometh a saint through the atonement of Christ the Lord, and becometh as a child, submissive, meek, humble, patient, full of love, willing to submit to all things which the Lord seeth fit to inflict upon him, even as a child doth submit to his father."[6]

We receive that change as we make and renew covenants with

God. That brings the power of Christ's Atonement to allow a transformation in our hearts. We can feel it every time we partake of the sacrament, perform a temple ordinance for a departed ancestor, testify as a witness of the Savior, or care for someone in need as Christ's disciple.

In those experiences, we become over time like a child in our capacity to love and obey. We come to stand on the sure foundation. Our faith in Jesus Christ brings us to repentance and to keeping His commandments. We obey, and we gain power to resist temptation, and we gain the promised companionship of the Holy Ghost.

Our natures change to become as a little child, obedient to God and more loving. That change will qualify us to enjoy the gifts that come through the Holy Ghost. Having the Spirit's companionship will comfort, guide, and strengthen us.

I have come to know some of what King Benjamin meant when he said that we could become like a little child before God. I have learned from many experiences that the Holy Ghost speaks most often in a quiet voice, heard most easily when one's heart is meek and submissive, like that of a child. In fact, the prayer that works is "I want only what You want. Just tell me what that is. I'll do it."

When the storms in life come, you can be steady because you are standing on the rock of your faith in Jesus Christ. That faith will lead you to daily repentance and consistent covenant keeping. Then you will always remember Him. And through the storms of hatred and wickedness, you will feel steady and hopeful.

More than that, you will find yourself reaching out to lift others to safety on the rock with you. Faith in Jesus Christ always leads to greater hope and to feelings of charity toward others, which is the true love of Christ.

I bear you my solemn witness that the Lord Jesus Christ has given you the invitation "Come unto me."[7] He invites you, out of love for you and for those you love, to come to Him for peace in this life and eternal life in the world to come. He knows perfectly the storms you will face in your test as part of the plan of happiness.

I plead with you to accept the Savior's invitation. Like a meek and loving child, accept His help. Make and keep the covenants He offers in The Church of Jesus Christ of Latter-day Saints. They will strengthen you. The Savior knows the storms and the places of safety on the way home to Him and to our Heavenly Father. He knows the way. He is the Way. I so testify in the sacred name of Jesus Christ, amen.

Notes

1. I have felt prompted to revisit a talk that I gave several years ago. For reference, see "As a Child," *Ensign* or *Liahona*, May 2006, 14–17.
2. 2 Timothy 3:1.
3. Helaman 5:12.
4. Mosiah 2:33, 38, 40.
5. Matthew 25:21.
6. Mosiah 3:19.
7. Matthew 11:28.

SATURDAY
AFTERNOON
SESSION

———

APRIL 2, 2022

FEAR NOT: BELIEVE ONLY!

ELDER JEFFREY R. HOLLAND

Of the Quorum of the Twelve Apostles

I direct my remarks today to the young people of the Church, meaning anyone President Russell M. Nelson's age or younger. I seldom use visuals, but I can't resist sharing this [photo of a letter from a young child].

This *cri de couer* comes from my eight-year-old friend Marin Arnold, written when she was seven. I will translate for you her early reformed Egyptian:

> *Dear Bishop*
> *generle confrins*
> *was Boring why*
> *Do we half to*
> *Do it? tell me why*
> *Sinserlie, Marin*
> *Arnold.*[1]

Well, Marin, the talk I am about to give will undoubtedly disappoint you again. But when you write your bishop to complain, it is important that you tell him my name is "Kearon. Elder Patrick Kearon."

For nearly two years a pandemic of biblical proportions has enveloped our planet, and while that plague brought a halt to almost everything socially, obviously it did not bring a halt to brutality, violence, and cruel aggression politically—nationally or internationally. As if that were not enough, we are still facing long-standing social and cultural challenges, ranging from economic deprivation to environmental desecration to racial inequity and more.

Such stiff winds and dark days can be discouraging to the youth among us, those to whom we look for optimism and enthusiasm regarding the tomorrows of our lives. It has been said that "the power of youth is the common wealth for the entire world. The . . . young . . . are the faces of our . . . future."[2] Furthermore, our children are the trustees into whose hands the destiny of this Church will be placed.

Given our current times, it is understandable if the idealism of the young is waning a little. Dr. Laurie Santos, a professor at Yale University, recently created a class titled *Psychology and the Good Life.* "The first year the class was offered, nearly [one-quarter] of the *[entire]* undergraduate student body enrolled."[3] Over 64 million people then visited her podcast. Writing about this phenomenon, one journalist noted how painful it is to see so many bright, young students—and adults—desperately "looking for something they've lost" or, worse yet, longing for something they never had.[4]

My plea today to our youth, and to you parents and adults who advise them, is to begin your search for happiness by embracing the bounty we have already received from the giver of every good gift.[5] At precisely the moment many in the world are asking deep questions of the soul, we ought to be answering with the "good news"[6] of the gospel of Jesus Christ. The Church of Jesus Christ of Latter-day Saints, which holds aloft the mission and message of the Savior of the world, offers the most eternally significant way to both find good and do good at such a needful time.

President Russell M. Nelson has said that this generation of young people has the capacity to have "more impact [for good] on the world than any previous generation."[7] We, of all people, should be "sing[ing] the song of redeeming love,"[8] but that takes discipline—"discipleship," if you will—the kind that guards against negative attitudes and destructive habits that would pull us off-key as we try to sing that song of eternal salvation.

Even as we stay "on the sunny side of the street,"[9] we do run into that fellow from time to time who is determined to find something bleak and dismal about everything. You know his motto: "It is always darkest just before it goes pitch-black." What a malignant vision, and what a miserable existence! Yes, we might sometimes want to run away from where we are, but we certainly should never run away from who we are—children of the living God who loves us, who is always ready to forgive us, and who will never, ever forsake us. You are His most precious possession. You are His child, to whom He has given prophets and promises, spiritual gifts and revelations, miracles and messages, and angels on both sides of the veil.[10]

He has also given you a church that strengthens families for mortality and binds them together for eternity. It provides more than 31,000 wards and branches where people gather and sing and fast and pray for each other and give of their means to the poor. This is where every person is named, accounted for, and ministered to and where lay friends and neighbors voluntarily serve each other in callings that range from clerical work to custodial duty. Young adults—and senior couples as well—serve missions by the thousands at their own expense with no say whatsoever as to where they will labor, and members young and old trundle off to temples to perform sacred ordinances necessary to bind the human family together—a bold activity in such a divided world but one which declares that such divisiveness is only temporary. These are a few of the reasons we give for "the hope that is in [us]."[11]

Of course, in our present day, tremendously difficult issues face any disciple of Jesus Christ. The leaders of this Church are giving their lives to seeking the Lord's guidance in the resolution of these challenges. If some are *not* resolved to the satisfaction of everyone, perhaps they constitute part of the cross Jesus said we would have to take up in order to follow Him.[12] It is precisely because there would be dark days and difficult issues that God promised He would, out of a cloud by day and a pillar of fire by night, guide prophets, give an iron rod, open a narrow gate leading to a strait path, and above all grant us the power to finish the course.[13]

So please, please, stay for the whole feast even if you are not sure about the broccoli. Bask in *His* light and lend *your* candle to the cause.[14] They have it right in Primary: Jesus really *does* "[want you] for a sunbeam."[15]

When the Jewish leader Jairus pled for Jesus to heal his 12-year-old daughter, who lay dying at home, the surrounding crowd waylaid the Savior so long that a servant soon came saying to this anxious father, "Thy daughter is dead; trouble not the Master."

"But when Jesus heard it, he answered him, saying, Fear not: believe only, and she shall be made whole."[16]

And she was. And so will you. "Fear not: believe only."

Because each of you in this audience is precious to God and to this Church, I close with this special apostolic declaration. Before you ever received the gift of the Holy Ghost, you had the Light of Christ planted in your soul,[17] that "light which is in all things, . . . giveth life to all things,"[18] and is the influence for good in the hearts of all people who have ever lived or ever will live. That light was given to protect you and teach you. One of its central messages is that life is the most precious of all gifts, a gift which is obtained eternally only through the Atonement of the Lord Jesus Christ. As the Light and Life of the World,[19] the Only Begotten Son of God came to give us life by conquering death.

We must commit ourselves fully to that gift of life and run to the aid of those who are at risk of giving up this sacred gift. Leaders, advisers, friends, family—watch for signs of depression, despair, or anything hinting of self-harm. Offer your help. Listen. Make some kind of intervention as appropriate.

To any of our youth out there who are struggling, whatever your concerns or difficulties, death by suicide is manifestly *not* the answer. It will not relieve the pain you are feeling or that you think you are causing. In a world that so desperately needs all the light it can get, please do *not* minimize the eternal light God put in *your* soul before this world was. Talk to someone. Ask for help. Do *not* destroy a life that Christ gave *His* life to preserve. You can bear the struggles of this mortal life because we will help you bear them. You are stronger than you think. Help *is* available, from others and especially from God. You are loved and valued and needed. We need you! "Fear not: believe only."

Someone who faced circumstances far more desperate than you and I ever will once cried: "Go forward [my beloved young friends]. Courage, . . . and on, on to the victory! Let your hearts rejoice, and be exceedingly glad."[20] We have so much to be glad about. We have each other, and we have Him. Don't deny us the chance to have you,

I plead, in the sacred and holy name of the Lord Jesus Christ, our Master, amen.

Notes

1. Marin Arnold, in email to Jeffrey R. Holland, Feb. 11, 2022, used with permission.
2. Kailash Satyarthi, in "Thoughts on Being Young," *Forbes India*, Feb. 25, 2021, forbesindia.com.
3. David Marchese, "Yale's Happiness Professor Says Anxiety Is Destroying Her Students," *New York Times Magazine*, Feb. 18, 2022, nytimes.com.
4. David Marchese, "Yale's Happiness Professor Says Anxiety Is Destroying Her Students."
5. See James 1:17; see also Moroni 10:5–20.
6. Bible Dictionary, "Gospels."
7. Russell M. Nelson, "A Personal Invitation to Participate in Seminary and Institute," Feb. 4, 2019, ChurchofJesusChrist.org.
8. Alma 5:26.
9. This phrase is taken from a 1930s popular jazz song titled "On the Sunny Side of the Street," with lyrics by Dorothy Fields (see "On the Sunny Side of the Street," Jazz Standards, jazzstandards.com).
10. See Jeffrey R. Holland, "The Ministry of Angels," *Ensign* or *Liahona*, Nov. 2008, 29–31.
11. 1 Peter 3:15.
12. See Matthew 16:24; Mark 10:21; Luke 9:23.
13. See, for example, Exodus 13:21–22; Amos 3:7; 1 Nephi 8:24, 30; 2 Nephi 9:41.
14. See Matthew 5:15–16; 3 Nephi 12:15–16.
15. "Jesus Wants Me for a Sunbeam," *Children's Songbook*, 60–61.
16. Luke 8:49–50; see also verses 41–42, 51–56.
17. See John 1:9; Doctrine and Covenants 93:2.
18. Doctrine and Covenants 88:13; see also verses 6–12.
19. See Mosiah 16:9; 3 Nephi 9:18; 11:11; Ether 4:12; see also John 8:12.
20. Doctrine and Covenants 128:22.

HE IS RISEN WITH HEALING IN HIS WINGS: WE CAN BE MORE THAN CONQUERORS

ELDER PATRICK KEARON

Of the Presidency of the Seventy

Marin, I'm Elder Holland, and things are about to go downhill.

We Are More Than Conquerors

We are all intrigued by survival stories. We hear tales of intrepid explorers and ordinary people alike who manage to keep themselves alive against all odds and expectations, and we can't help but ask ourselves, "Could I have done that?"

I think immediately of British explorer Ernest Shackleton and the crew of his ship HMS *Endurance*, shipwrecked in Antarctic ice and then stranded on a barren island for nearly two years. Shackleton's extraordinary leadership and indomitable resolve saved the lives of his men, despite the harshest conditions.

Then I think of the crew of Apollo 13 hurtling through space to land on the moon! But disaster struck when an oxygen tank exploded, and the mission had to be aborted. Short of oxygen, the crew and mission control ingeniously improvised and brought all three astronauts safely back to earth.

I marvel at the astonishing survival of individuals and families victimized by war, imprisoned in camps, and those who become refugees who heroically and courageously keep alive the flame of hope for fellow sufferers, who impart goodness in the face of brutality, and who somehow manage to help others endure just one more day.

Could you or I survive in any one of these extreme circumstances?

Perhaps some of you, however, consider the accounts of survivors, and your soul cries out that *you are* living a survival story *right now* as a victim of abuse, neglect, bullying, domestic violence, or any suffering of this kind. You are in the midst of your own desperate attempt to survive a situation that feels very much like a disastrous shipwreck or a promising mission suddenly aborted. Will you ever be rescued; will you make it through your own survival story?

The answer is *yes*. You can survive. You have in fact already been rescued; you have already been saved—by the One who has suffered the very torment you are suffering and endured the very agony you are enduring.[1] Jesus has overcome the abuses of this world[2] to give you power to not only *survive* but one day, through Him, to overcome and even *conquer*—to completely rise above the pain, the misery, the anguish, and see them replaced by peace.

The Apostle Paul asks:

"Who shall separate us from the love of Christ? shall tribulation, or distress, or persecution, or famine, or nakedness, or peril, or sword? . . .

"Nay, in *all* these things we are *more than conquerors through him that loved us*."[3]

The Promises to Covenant Israel

You will remember when President Russell M. Nelson issued the following invitation in general conference. He said: "As you study your scriptures . . . , I encourage you to make a list of all that the Lord has promised He will do for covenant Israel. I think you will be astounded!"[4]

Here are just a few of the powerful and comforting promises our family found. Imagine the Lord speaking these words to you—to *you* who are surviving—because they *are* for you:

Fear not.[5]

I know your sorrows, and I have come to deliver you.[6]

I will not leave you.[7]

My name is upon you, and my angels have charge over you.[8]

I will do wonders among you.[9]

Walk with me; learn of me; I will give you rest.[10]

I am in your midst.[11]

You are mine.[12]

To Those Who Are Surviving

With those assurances very much in mind, I want to speak directly to those who feel as though there is no way out of their own survival story because of the trauma inflicted by the cruel actions of others. If this is your survival story, we weep with you. We yearn for you to overcome the confusion, shame, and fear, and we long for you, through Jesus Christ, to *conquer*.

From Victim to Survivor to Conqueror

If you have experienced any kind of abuse, violence, or oppression, you may be left with the idea that these events were somehow your fault and that you deserve to carry the shame and guilt you feel. You may have had thoughts such as:

- I could have prevented this.
- God doesn't love me anymore.
- Nobody will ever love me.
- I am damaged beyond repair.
- The Savior's Atonement applies to others but not to me.

These erroneous thoughts and feelings may have been a barrier to seeking help from family, friends, leaders, or professionals, and so you have struggled alone. If you have sought help from those you trust, you may still be wrestling with ideas of shame and even self-loathing. The impact of these events can remain for many years. You hope that one day you'll feel better, but somehow that day has not yet come.

The abuse was not, is not, and never will be your fault, no matter what the abuser or anyone else may have said to the contrary. When you have been a victim of cruelty, incest, or any other perversion, you are not the one who needs to repent; you are not responsible.

You are not less worthy or less valuable or less loved as a human being, or as a daughter or son of God, because of what someone else has done to you.

God does not now see, nor has He ever seen, you as someone to be despised. Whatever has happened to you, He is *not* ashamed of you or disappointed in you. He loves you in a way you have yet to discover. And you *will* discover it as you trust in His promises and as you learn to believe Him when He says you are "*precious* in [His] sight."[13]

You are not defined by these terrible things that have been done to you. You are, in glorious truth, defined by your eternally existing identity as a son or daughter of God and by your Creator's perfect, infinite love and invitation to whole and complete healing.

Though it may seem impossible, feel impossible, healing *can* come through the miracle of the redemptive might of the Atonement of Jesus Christ, who is risen "with healing in his wings."[14]

Our merciful Savior, victorious over darkness and depravity, has power to right *all* wrongs, a life-giving truth for those wronged by others.[15]

Please know that the Savior has descended below *all* things, even what has happened to you. Because of that, He knows exactly what real terror and shame feel like and how it feels to be abandoned and broken.[16] From the depths of His atoning suffering, the Savior imparts hope you thought was lost forever, strength you believed you could never possess, and healing you couldn't imagine was possible.

Abusive Behavior Is Explicitly Condemned by the Lord and by His Prophets

There is no place for any kind of abuse—physical, sexual, emotional, or verbal—in any home, any country, or any culture. Nothing a wife, child, or husband might do or say makes them "deserve" to be beaten. No one, in any country or culture, is ever "asking for" aggression or violence from someone else in authority or by someone who is bigger and stronger.

Those who abuse and who seek to hide their grievous sins may get away with it for a time. But the Lord, who sees all, knows the deeds and the thoughts and intents of the heart.[17] He is a God of justice, and His divine justice will be served.[18]

Miraculously, the Lord is also a God of mercy to the truly repentant. Abusers—including those who were once abused themselves—who confess, forsake their sin, and do *all* in their power to make recompense and restitution, have access to forgiveness through the miracle of the Atonement of Christ.

For the falsely accused, the unspeakable gravity of these accusations brings its own purgatory. But they too are blessed by the Savior's vicarious suffering for them and the knowledge that ultimately truth will prevail.

But unrepentant abusers will stand before the Lord to account for their heinous crimes.

The Lord Himself is crystal clear in His condemnation of abuse of any kind: "But whoso shall offend one of these little ones . . . , it were better for him that a millstone were hanged about his neck, and that he were drowned in the depth of the sea."[19]

Conclusion

Dear friends who have been so terribly wounded—and for that matter, anyone who has borne the injustices of life—you can have a new beginning and a fresh start. In Gethsemane and on Calvary, Jesus "took upon Himself . . . *all* of the anguish and suffering *ever* experienced by you and me,"[20] and He has overcome it all! With arms outstretched, the Savior offers the gift of healing to you. With courage, patience, and faithful focus on Him, before too long you can come to fully accept this gift. You can let go of your pain and leave it at His feet.

Your gentle Savior declared, "The thief cometh not, but for to steal, and to kill, and to destroy: I am come that [you] might have life, and that [you] might have it more abundantly."[21] You are a survivor, you can heal, and you can trust that with the power and grace of Jesus Christ, you will overcome and conquer.

Jesus specializes in the seemingly impossible. He came here to make the impossible possible, the irredeemable redeemable, to heal the unhealable, to right the unrightable, to promise the unpromisable.[22] And He's really good at it. In fact, He's perfect at it. In the name of Jesus Christ, our Healer, amen.

Notes

1. See Alma 7:11–12. President Russell M. Nelson taught: "[Jesus Christ] was brutally reviled, mocked, spit upon, and scourged. In the Garden of Gethsemane, our Savior took upon Himself *every* pain, *every* sin, and *all* of the anguish and suffering *ever* experienced by you and me and by everyone who has ever lived or will ever live. Under the weight of that excruciating burden, He bled from every pore [see Doctrine and Covenants 19:18]. All of this suffering was intensified as He was cruelly crucified on Calvary's cross" ("The Correct Name of the Church," *Ensign* or *Liahona*, Nov. 2018, 88).
2. See John 16:33; Philippians 4:13.
3. Romans 8:35, 37; emphasis added.
4. Russell M. Nelson, "Let God Prevail," *Ensign* or *Liahona*, Nov. 2020, 95.
5. See Isaiah 41:10; 2 Nephi 8:7.
6. See Exodus 3:7–8.
7. See Deuteronomy 31:6.
8. See Doctrine and Covenants 109:22.
9. See Joshua 3:5.
10. See Matthew 11:28; Doctrine and Covenants 19:23; Moses 6:34.
11. See Doctrine and Covenants 38:7.
12. See Isaiah 43:1.
13. Isaiah 43:4; emphasis added.
14. Malachi 4:2.
15. Elder Dale G. Renlund testified that "all that is unfair about life can be made right through the Atonement of Jesus Christ" ("Infuriating Unfairness," *Liahona*, May 2021, 43); see also *Preach My Gospel: A Guide to Missionary Service* [2019], 52; Isaiah 61:1–3; Revelation 21:4).
16. See Doctrine and Covenants 88:6; 122:5–8.
17. See Alma 18:32; 39:8.
18. See 2 Nephi 9:17; Doctrine and Covenants 1:1–3.
19. Matthew 18:6. "The terrible, vicious practice of sexual abuse . . . is beyond understanding. . . . It is a violation of that which is sacred and divine. . . . It is reprehensible and worthy of the most severe condemnation. Shame on any man or woman who would sexually abuse a child. In doing so, the abuser not only does the most serious kind of injury. He or she also stands condemned before the Lord" (Gordon B. Hinckley, "Save the Children," *Ensign*, Nov. 1994, 54).
20. Russell M. Nelson, "The Correct Name of the Church," 88.
21. John 10:10.
22. See Luke 4:16–19.

LIFT UP YOUR HEART AND REJOICE

ELDER MARCOS A. AIDUKAITIS
Of the Seventy

Speaking to Thomas B. Marsh, a recent convert, the Lord said encouragingly, "Lift up your heart and rejoice, for the hour of your mission is come" (Doctrine and Covenants 31:3).

I believe this invitation can serve as an inspiration for all members of the Church. After all, we have each received from our Heavenly Father the mission of gathering Israel on both sides of the veil.

"That gathering," President Russell M. Nelson has said, "is the most important thing taking place on earth today. Nothing else compares in magnitude, nothing else compares in importance, nothing else compares in majesty."[1]

Certainly, there are many worthy causes in the world. It is impossible to name them all. But wouldn't you like to participate in a great cause within your reach and where your contribution makes a vital difference? The gathering makes an eternal difference to all. People of all ages can participate in this cause regardless of their circumstances and where they live. There is no other cause in the world more inclusive.

Speaking specifically to the youth, President Nelson said that "our Heavenly Father has reserved many of His most noble spirits—perhaps . . . His finest team—for this final phase. Those noble spirits—those finest players, those heroes—are *you*!"[2]

Yes, you have been prepared from before this life and born now to participate in the great work of the gathering of Israel on both sides of the veil in these latter days (see Doctrine and Covenants 138:53–56).

Why is this cause so important? Because "the worth of souls is great in the sight of God" (Doctrine and Covenants 18:10). And because "whoso believeth in [Jesus Christ], and is baptized, the same shall be saved; and . . . shall inherit the kingdom of God" (3 Nephi 11:33). Furthermore, "all that [the] Father hath shall be given unto" those who receive His ordinances and keep His covenants (Doctrine and Covenants 84:38). In addition, "the labourers are few" (Luke 10:2).

Only in The Church of Jesus Christ of Latter-day Saints do we find the power, the authority, and the way to offer such a blessing to others, whether living or dead.

As President Nelson said: "*Anytime* you do *anything* that helps *anyone*—on either side of the veil—take a step toward making covenants with God and receiving their essential baptismal and temple ordinances, you are helping to gather Israel. It is as simple as that."[3]

While there are many ways to help in the gathering, I would like to speak of one in particular: serving as a full-time missionary. For many of you, this will mean being a teaching missionary. For many others, it will mean being a service missionary. But the world tries to distract youth from this most sacred responsibility using fear and insecurities.

Some other distractions might be experiencing a pandemic, leaving a good job, putting off education, or being particularly interested in someone romantically. Everyone will have his or her own set of challenges. Such distractions can arise at precisely the time of embarking in the service of the Lord, and choices that seem obvious later are not always as easy in the moment.

I know from experience the troubled mind of such a young person. When I was preparing to go on my mission, some surprising forces tried to discourage me. One was my dentist. When he realized my appointment was so I could be a missionary, he tried to dissuade me from serving. I had not had the least notion that my dentist was against the Church.

The interruption of my education was also complicated. When I asked for a two-year leave of absence from my university program, I was informed that it was not possible. I would lose my place at the university if I did not return after one year. In Brazil, this was serious since the only criterion for admittance in a university program was a very difficult and competitive examination.

After repeatedly insisting, I was reluctantly informed that after being absent for one year, I could apply for an exception on extraordinary grounds. It might be approved or not. I was terrified at the idea of retaking that difficult admissions test after two years away from my studies.

I also was especially interested in a young woman. Several of my friends shared that same interest. I thought to myself, "If I go on a mission, I'm running a risk."

But the Lord Jesus Christ was my great inspiration not to be afraid of the future as I strove to serve Him with all my heart.

He also had a mission to fulfill. In His own words, He explained, "For I came down from heaven, not to do mine own will, but the will of him that sent me" (John 6:38). And was His mission easy? Of course not. His suffering, which was an essential part of His mission, caused Him, "even God, the greatest of all, to tremble because of pain, and to bleed at every pore, and to suffer both body and spirit—and would that [He] might not drink the bitter cup, and shrink—

"Nevertheless, glory be to the Father, and [He] partook and finished [His] preparations unto the children of men" (Doctrine and Covenants 19:18–19).

Serving a full-time mission may seem difficult to us. Perhaps it requires that we give up important things for a moment. The Lord certainly knows this, and He will always be by our side.

In fact, in their message to missionaries in *Preach My Gospel*, the First Presidency promises, "The Lord will reward and richly bless you as you humbly and prayerfully serve Him."[4] It is true that all the children of God are blessed in one way or another, but there is a difference between being blessed and being richly blessed in His service.

Remember the challenges that I thought I faced prior to my mission? My dentist? I found another. My university? They made an exception for me. Remember that young woman? She married one of my good friends.

But God truly blessed me richly. And I learned that the blessings of the Lord can come in ways different from how we expect. After all, His thoughts are not our thoughts (see Isaiah 55:8–9).

Among the many rich blessings He has given me for serving Him as a full-time missionary are a greater faith in Jesus Christ and His Atonement and a stronger knowledge and testimony of His teachings, so that I am not easily swayed by "every wind of doctrine" (Ephesians 4:14). I lost my fear of teaching. My capacity to face challenges with optimism increased. By observing individuals and families I met or taught as a missionary, I learned that the teachings of God are true when He says that sin does not bring true happiness and that obedience to the commandments of God helps us prosper both temporally and spiritually (see Mosiah 2:41; Alma 41:10). And I learned for myself that God is a God of miracles (see Mormon 9).

All of these things were instrumental in my preparation for adult life, including possible marriage and parenthood, Church service, and professional and community life.

After my mission, I benefited from my increased courage to present myself as a faithful follower of Jesus Christ and His Church in all circumstances and to all people, even sharing the gospel with a beautiful woman who would become my virtuous, wise, fun, and beloved eternal companion, the sunshine of my life.

Yes, God has blessed me richly, far beyond what I imagined, just as He will all those who "humbly and prayerfully serve Him." I am eternally grateful to God for His goodness.

My mission completely shaped my life. I learned it is worth the effort to trust in God, to trust in His wisdom and mercy and in His promises. After all, He is our Father, and without any doubt, He wants the best for us.

Dear youth throughout the world, I extend the same invitation that our prophet, President Nelson, has made to all of you "to enlist in the youth battalion of the Lord to help gather Israel." President Nelson said:

"There is *nothing* of greater consequence. Absolutely *nothing*.

"This gathering should mean *everything* to you. This *is* the mission for which you were sent to earth."[5]

We were born at this time for a divine purpose, the gathering of Israel. When we serve as full-time missionaries, we will be challenged at times, but the Lord Himself is our great exemplar and guide in such circumstances. He understands what a difficult mission is. With His help, we can do hard things. He will be by our side (see Doctrine and Covenants 84:88), and He will bless us greatly as we humbly serve Him.

For all these reasons, I am not surprised that the Lord said to Thomas B. Marsh and to all of us, "Lift up your heart and rejoice, for the hour of your mission is come." In the name of Jesus Christ, amen.

Notes

1. Russell M. Nelson, "Hope of Israel" (worldwide youth devotional, June 3, 2018), HopeofIsrael .ChurchofJesusChrist.org.
2. Russell M. Nelson, "Hope of Israel."
3. Russell M. Nelson, "Hope of Israel."
4. *Preach My Gospel: A Guide to Missionary Service* (2019), v.
5. Russell M. Nelson, "Hope of Israel."

WE EACH HAVE A STORY

ELDER GERRIT W. GONG
Of the Quorum of the Twelve Apostles

Friends, brothers and sisters, we each have a story. As we discover our story, we connect, we belong, we become.

My name is Gerrit Walter Gong. Gerrit is a Dutch name, Walter (my father's name) is an American name, and Gong of course is a Chinese name.

Experts estimate some 70–110 billion people have lived on the earth. Perhaps only one has been named Gerrit Walter Gong.

We each have a story. I love "the rain on my face [and] the wind as it rushes by."[1] I wobble-waddle with penguins in Antarctica. I give orphans in Guatemala, street kids in Cambodia, Maasai women in the African Mara their first very own photo of themselves.

I wait at the hospital as each of our children is born—once the doctor has me help.

I trust God. I believe "[we] are, that [we] might have joy,"[2] that there are times and seasons to everything under heaven.[3]

Do you know your story? What your name means? World population grew from 1.1 billion people in 1820 to nearly 7.8 billion in 2020.[4] The year 1820 seems to be an inflection point in history. Many born after 1820 have living memory and records to identify several family generations. Can you think of a special, sweet memory with a grandparent or other family member?

Whatever the total number of individuals who have lived on the earth, it is finite, countable, one person at a time. You and I, we each matter.

And please consider this: whether or not we know them, we are each born of a mother and father. And each mother and father is born of a mother and father.[5] By birth or adoptive lineage, we are ultimately all connected in the family of God and in the human family.

Born AD 837, my 30th great-grandfather, First Dragon Gong, started our family village in southern China. The first time I visited

Gong village, the people said, *"Wenhan huilaile"* ("Gerrit has returned").

On my mother's side, our living family tree includes thousands of family names, with more to discover.[6] We each have more family with whom to connect. If you think your great-aunt has completed all your family genealogy, please find your cousins and cousins' cousins. Connect your living memory family names with the 10 billion searchable names FamilySearch now has in its online collection and the 1.3 billion individuals in its Family Tree.[7]

Ask friends or family to draw a living tree. As President Russell M. Nelson teaches, living trees have roots *and* branches.[8] Whether you are your first or tenth known generation, connect yesterday for tomorrow. Connect the roots and branches in your living family tree.[9]

The question "Where are you from?" asks lineage, birthplace, and home country or homeland. Globally, 25 percent of us trace our homeland to China, 23 percent to India, 17 percent to other parts of Asia and the Pacific, 18 percent to Europe, 10 percent to Africa, 7 percent to the Americas.[10]

The question "Where are you from?" also invites us to discover our divine identity and spiritual purpose in life.

We each have a story.

A family I know connected five family generations when they visited their old home in Winnipeg, Canada. There the grandfather told his grandsons about the day two missionaries (he called them angels from heaven) brought the restored gospel of Jesus Christ, changing their family forever.

A mother I know invited her children and their cousins to ask their great-grandmother about her childhood experiences. Great-Grandma's adventures and life lessons are now a treasured family book uniting generations.

A young man I know is compiling a "Dad journal." Years ago, a car hit and killed his father. Now, to know his father, this courageous young man is preserving childhood memories and stories from family and friends.

When asked where meaning comes in life, most people rank

family first.[11] This includes family living and gone before. Of course, when we die, we don't cease to exist. We continue to live on the other side of the veil.

Still very much alive, our ancestors deserve to be remembered.[12] We remember our heritage through oral histories, clan records and family stories, memorials or places of remembrance, and celebrations with photos, foods, or items which remind us of loved ones.

Think of where you live—isn't it wonderful how your country and community remember and honor ancestors, family, others who served and sacrificed? For example, at the autumn harvest remembrance in South Molton, Devonshire, England, Sister Gong and I loved finding the little church and community where generations of our Bawden family lived. We honor our ancestors by opening the heavens through temple and family history work[13] and by becoming a welding link[14] in the chain of our generations.[15]

In this age of "I choose me," societies benefit when generations connect in meaningful ways. We need roots to have wings—real relationships, meaningful service, life beyond fleeting social media veneers.

Connecting with our ancestors can change our lives in surprising ways. From their trials and accomplishments, we gain faith and strength.[16] From their love and sacrifices, we learn to forgive and move forward. Our children become resilient. We gain protection and power. Ties with ancestors increase family closeness, gratitude, miracles. Such ties can bring help from the other side of the veil.

Just as joys come in families, so can sorrows. No individual is perfect, nor is any family. When those who should love, nurture, and protect us fail to do so, we feel abandoned, embarrassed, hurt. Family can become a hollow shell. Yet, with heaven's help, we can come to understand our family and make peace with each other.[17]

Sometimes unwavering commitment to abiding family relationships helps us accomplish hard things. In some cases, community becomes family. A remarkable young woman whose troubled family moved frequently found a loving Church family wherever she was to nurture and give her place. Genetics and family patterns influence but do not determine us.

God wants our families to be happy and forever. Forever is too long if we make each other unhappy. Happy is too short if cherished relationships stop with this life. Through sacred covenants, Jesus Christ offers His love, power, and grace to change us[18] and heal our relationships. Selfless temple service for dear ones makes our Savior's Atonement real for them and us. Sanctified, we can return home to God's presence as families united eternally.[19]

Each of our stories is a journey still in progress, as we discover, create, and become with possibilities beyond imagination.

The Prophet Joseph Smith said, "It may seem to some to be a very bold doctrine that we talk of—a power which records or binds on earth and binds in heaven."[20] The sociality we create here can exist with eternal glory there.[21] Indeed, "we without [our family members] cannot be made perfect; neither can they without us be made perfect," that is, in "a whole and complete and perfect union."[22]

What can we do now?

First, imagine your image reflected back and forth between two mirrors of eternity. In one direction, picture yourself as daughter, granddaughter, great-granddaughter; in the other direction, smile at yourself as aunt, mother, grandmother. How quickly time passes! In each time and role, notice who is with you. Gather their photos and stories; make their memories real. Record their names, experiences, key dates. They are your family—the family you have and the family you want.

As you perform temple ordinances for family members, the spirit of Elijah, "a manifestation of the Holy Ghost bearing witness of the divine nature of the family,"[23] will knit the hearts of your fathers, mothers, and children together in love.[24]

Second, let the adventure of family history be intentional and spontaneous. Call your grandmother. Look deeply into the eyes of that new baby. Make time—discover eternity—at each stage of your journey. Learn and acknowledge with gratitude and honesty your family heritage. Celebrate and become the positive and, where needed, humbly do everything possible not to pass on the negative. Let good things begin with you.

Third, visit FamilySearch.org. Download the available mobile apps. They're free and fun. Discover, connect, belong. See how you are related to people in a room, how easy and rewarding it is to add names to your living family tree, to find and bless your roots and branches.

Fourth, help unite families eternally. Remember the demographics of heaven. There are many more on the other side of the veil than on this side. As more temples come closer to us, please offer those waiting for temple ordinances opportunity to receive them.

The promise at Easter and always is that, in and through Jesus Christ, we can become our best story and our families can become happy and forever. In all our generations, Jesus Christ heals the brokenhearted, delivers the captives, sets at liberty them that are bruised.[25] Covenant belonging with God and each other[26] includes knowing our spirit and body will be reunited in resurrection and our most precious relationships can continue beyond death with a fulness of joy.[27]

We each have a story. Come discover yours. Come find your voice, your song, your harmony in Him. This is the very purpose for which God created the heavens and the earth and saw that they were good.[28]

Praise God's plan of happiness, Jesus Christ's Atonement, continuing restoration in His gospel and Church. Please come find your family, all your generations, and bring them home. In the sacred and holy name of Jesus Christ, amen.

Notes

1. "My Heavenly Father Loves Me," *Children's Songbook*, 228.
2. 2 Nephi 2:25.
3. See Ecclesiastes 3:1.
4. Based on United Nations Secretariat, *The World at Six Billion* (1999), 5, table 1; "World Population by Year," Worldometer, worldometers.info.
5. Many are blessed to have parents who did not physically bear them, yet they are joined as family through bonds of affection and adoption and sacred sealing covenants.
6. I express appreciation to those who are piloting ways to organize large numbers of family names into family trees.
7. In 2021, some 99 million names were added to public family trees. And recently, digitization

was completed of 2.4 million rolls of microfilm containing approximately 37 billion names (with some duplications). These individual name records can now be prepared to be searched, found, and added to the family tree of humanity.

8. See Russell M. Nelson, "Roots and Branches," *Ensign* or *Liahona*, May 2004, 27–29.

9. Of course, as we discover and build our living family tree, please maintain 100 percent respect for the privacy and volunteer participation of family members, living and deceased.

10. David Quimette extrapolated these numbers, based on Angus Maddison, *The World Economy: A Millennial Perspective* (2001), 241, table B-10.

11. See Laura Silver and others, "What Makes Life Meaningful? Views from 17 Advanced Economies," Pew Research Center, Nov. 18, 2021, pewresearch.org.

12. 1 Nephi 9:5; 1 Nephi 19:3; Words of Mormon 1:6–7; and Alma 37:2 speak of keeping records and remembering "for a wise purpose," including to bless future generations.

13. See Russell M. Nelson and Wendy W. Nelson, "Open the Heavens through Temple and Family History Work," *Ensign*, Oct. 2017, 34–39; *Liahona*, Oct. 2017, 14–19; see also "RootsTech Family Discovery Day—Opening Session 2017" (video), ChurchofJesusChrist.org.

14. See Doctrine and Covenants 128:18.

15. See Gordon B. Hinckley, "Keep the Chain Unbroken" (Brigham Young University devotional, Nov. 30, 1999), speeches.byu.edu. President Hinckley is also quoted in David A. Bednar, "A Welding Link" (worldwide devotional for young adults, Sept. 10, 2017), broadcasts .ChurchofJesusChrist.org.

16. For example, in our family, Henry Bawden, from Devonshire, England, married Sarah Howard, who emigrated with her family after they joined the Church. While Sarah was in St. Louis as a young teenager, her father, mother, and five siblings died. Henry and Sarah had 10 children. Sarah also raised six children of Henry's first wife, Ann Ireland, after she died. Sarah was also mother to two young granddaughters after her (Sarah's) daughter-in-law passed away. Despite life's many challenges, Sarah was warm, loving, compassionate, and of course very hardworking. She was affectionately known as "Little Grandma."

17. Hard as it may be, as we forgive ourselves and each other with Christ's help, we become "the children of God" (Matthew 5:9).

18. See, for example, Mosiah 3:19.

19. See "The Family: A Proclamation to the World," ChurchofJesusChrist.org.

20. Doctrine and Covenants 128:9.

21. See Doctrine and Covenants 130:2.

22. Doctrine and Covenants 128:18.

23. Russell M. Nelson, "A New Harvest Time," *Ensign*, May 1998, 34; see also Russell M. Nelson and Wendy W. Nelson, "Open the Heavens through Temple and Family History Work," 16–18.

24. See Mosiah 18:21.

25. See Luke 4:18.

26. I am told the Hebrew word for family—*mishpachah*—comes from a Hebrew root word (*shaphahh*) meaning "to join or bind together." Every role within the family is designed to strengthen family bonds.

27. See Doctrine and Covenants 88:15–16, 34; 93:33; 138:17.

28. See Genesis 1:4, 31.

IS THE PLAN WORKING?

ELDER ADRIÁN OCHOA

Of the Seventy

Is the plan working?

Recently I had a conversation with a young adult who served a mission several years ago and was now involved in his professional work. In some ways, his life was going well. But his faith was in decline. He was sinking into a sea of doubt about the Savior and His Church. He explained that he wasn't receiving the blessings he expected from the restored gospel. He didn't feel that the plan of happiness was working in his life.

My message today is for all those who might have similar feelings. I speak to those who at one time "felt to sing the song of redeeming love" but do not "feel so now."[1]

Our Heavenly Father has prepared a wonderful plan for our eternal happiness. But when life does not unfold the way we hoped, it might seem that the plan is not working.

Perhaps we feel the way Jesus's disciples felt when they were in a ship "in the midst of the sea, tossed with waves: for the wind was contrary."[2]

Then, very early in the morning:

"Jesus went unto them, walking on the sea.

"And when the disciples saw him walking on the sea, they were troubled, . . . and they cried out for fear.

"But straightway Jesus spake unto them, saying, Be of good cheer; it is I; be not afraid.

"And Peter answered him and said, Lord, if it be thou, bid me come unto thee on the water.

"And he said, Come. And when Peter was come down out of the ship, he walked on the water, to go to Jesus.

"But when he saw the wind boisterous, he was afraid; and beginning to sink, he cried, . . . Lord, save me.

"And immediately Jesus stretched forth his hand, and caught

him, and said unto him, O thou of little faith, wherefore didst thou doubt?"[3]

Could I share with you three principles I learn from Peter? I pray that these principles might help anyone who feels that the plan of happiness isn't working in their lives.

First, act in faith in Jesus Christ.

I am in awe of Peter's faith. At Jesus's simple invitation to "come," he left his storm-tossed ship. He seemed to know that if Jesus Christ invited him to do something, he could do it.[4] Peter trusted the Savior more than he trusted his boat. And that faith gave him power to act with courage during a stressful, frightening situation.

Peter's faith reminds me of an experience that I heard from Elder José L. Alonso. Shortly after Elder Alonso's son passed away, leaving a family with young children, Elder Alonso overheard the children talking.

"What are we going to do?" they asked.

A nine-year-old daughter answered, "Daddy is OK. He is preaching the gospel of Jesus Christ."

Like Peter, this little girl saw beyond her challenges and trusted in Jesus Christ and His Atonement. Faith in the Savior brings peace and the strength to move forward.

If you look back on your life, I believe you will see that you have exercised faith many times. Joining the Church is an act of faith. Speaking with Heavenly Father in prayer is an act of faith. Reading the scriptures is an act of faith. Listening to my message in this general conference is an act of faith. As President Russell M. Nelson has said, "Do not minimize the faith you already have."[5]

Another lesson I learn from Peter is this:

In times of trouble, turn to Jesus Christ right away.

As he walked toward the Savior, Peter was frightened by the wind and began to sink. But when Peter realized what was happening, he did not try to tread water on his own or swim back to the ship. Rather than let go of his faith in Christ, he held on more tightly, crying, "Lord, save me."

"And immediately Jesus stretched forth his hand, and caught him."[6]

All of us face boisterous winds that can shake our faith and cause us to sink. When this happens, please remember that Heavenly Father's plan of happiness has another name—the plan of redemption. The plan was not for us to glide easily through life, never stumbling, never sinking, with a smile always on our face. Heavenly Father knew that we would need to be redeemed. This is why He prepared the plan of redemption.[7] This is why He sent a Redeemer. When we struggle—for any reason—that does not mean the plan isn't working. That is when we need the plan the most!

In those moments, follow the example of Peter. Turn to the Savior right away.

"Now is the time and the day of your salvation. . . . Do not procrastinate the day of your repentance."[8]

No matter where we are and where we have been, repentance is the way forward. President Nelson has taught:

"Nothing is more liberating, more ennobling, or more crucial to our individual progression than is a regular, daily focus on repentance. . . .

"Whether you are diligently moving along the covenant path, have slipped or stepped from the covenant path, or can't even see the path from where you are now, I plead with you to repent. Experience the strengthening power of daily repentance—of doing and being a little better each day."[9]

Coming unto Christ means more than just thinking about Him or talking about Him or even loving Him. It means following Him. It means living the way He teaches us to live. And for all of us, that means repenting, without delay.

One of my daughters used to work at the missionary training center. She told me of an elder she taught who confided in her that he wasn't sure the Book of Mormon was true. He had prayed and prayed for a spiritual witness, but he received no answer.

My daughter prayed to know what she should do to help this missionary. The impression she received was that the scriptures were not given only so we can read them and obtain a testimony; they were given also to teach us to keep the commandments of God. My daughter shared this thought with the missionary.

Later, she saw this missionary again, looking much happier. He told her that he had finally received a testimony that the Book of Mormon is true. He knew that this witness came because he was making a greater effort to *do* what the Book of Mormon teaches.

Let us follow Peter's example of turning to the Savior during times of trouble. Follow Jesus Christ instead of relying on your own wisdom and strength. No matter how long you've been trying to tread water without Him, it's never too late to reach out to Him. The plan works!

A third principle I learn from Peter and his experience is this:

Humble yourself before the Lord, and He will lift you up to greater things.

Peter had shown faith, both in walking on the water and in reaching out to the Savior when he needed help. Even so, the Savior saw in Peter the potential for so much more. "O thou of little faith," He said, "wherefore didst thou doubt?"[10]

Peter could have resented this rebuke. But he accepted it humbly. He continued to seek greater faith in Jesus Christ. Through many additional faith-building experiences—some of them very, very difficult—Peter eventually became the rock-solid leader the Lord needed him to be. He accomplished great things in the Lord's service.

What great things does the Lord want you to accomplish? In His Church and kingdom, there are many opportunities to serve and minister to others as the Savior did. He wants you to be part of His great work. Never will the plan of happiness become more real to you than when you are helping others to live it.

In building my own faith, these words of Alma were life-changing: "Blessed are they who humble themselves without being compelled to be humble."[11] Let us humbly put ourselves in a position where Jesus can lift us, lead us, and make the most of our abilities.[12]

I testify that the plan of happiness works. It was created by your Heavenly Father, who loves you. It works because Jesus Christ overcame sin and death through His Atonement. Come unto Him, follow Him, and "immediately shall the great plan of redemption be brought about unto you."[13] In the name of Jesus Christ, amen.

Notes

1. Alma 5:26.
2. Matthew 14:24. There are many things about modern life that are contrary to the ways of a disciple of Jesus Christ. We live in the day that the Savior predicted, when "all things shall be in commotion; and surely, men's hearts shall fail them" (Doctrine and Covenants 88:91; see also Doctrine and Covenants 45:26).
3. Matthew 14:25–31.
4. See 1 Nephi 3:7.
5. Russell M. Nelson, "Christ Is Risen; Faith in Him Will Move Mountains," *Liahona*, May 2021, 104.
6. Matthew 14:30–31.
7. Elder Lynn G. Robbins taught: "Repentance is God's ever-accessible gift that allows and enables us to go from failure to failure without any loss of enthusiasm. Repentance isn't His backup plan in the event we might fail. Repentance *is* His plan, knowing that we will. This is the gospel of repentance" ("Until Seventy Times Seven," *Ensign* or *Liahona*, May 2018, 22).
8. Alma 34:31, 33.
9. Russell M. Nelson, "We Can Do Better and Be Better," *Ensign* or *Liahona*, May 2019, 67.
10. Matthew 14:31.
11. Alma 32:16.
12. The Lord has said, "No one can assist in this work except he shall be humble and full of love" (Doctrine and Covenants 12:8).
13. Alma 34:31.

"THEN WILL I MAKE WEAK THINGS BECOME STRONG"

ELDER KEVIN S. HAMILTON
Of the Seventy

President Thomas S. Monson once shared the story of prison warden Clinton Duffy. "During the 1940s and 1950s, [Warden Duffy] was well known for his efforts to rehabilitate the men in his prison. Said one critic, 'You should know that leopards don't change their spots!'

"Replied Warden Duffy, 'You should know I don't work with leopards. I work with men, and men change every day.'"[1]

One of Satan's greatest lies is that men and women cannot change. This untruth gets told and retold in many different ways as the world says that we simply cannot change—or worse yet, that we should not change. We are taught that our circumstances define us. We should "embrace who we really are," the world says, "and be authentic to our true selves."

We Can Change

While it is indeed good to be authentic, we should be authentic to our real, true selves as sons and daughters of God with a divine nature and destiny to become like Him.[2] If our goal is to be authentic to this divine nature and destiny, then we will all need to change. The scriptural word for change is *repentance*. "Too many people," President Russell M. Nelson teaches, "consider repentance as punishment—something to be avoided except in the most serious circumstances. . . . When Jesus asks you and me to 'repent,' He is inviting us to change."[3]

God's Conditions

Computer software developers use conditional statements to tell computers what to do. These are sometimes referred to as if-then statements. As in, if x is true, then do y.

The Lord also operates through conditions: conditions of faith, conditions of righteousness, conditions of repentance. There are many examples of conditional statements from God such as:

"*If* you keep my commandments and endure to the end [*then*] you shall have eternal life, which gift is the greatest of all the gifts of God."[4]

Or "*if* ye shall ask with a sincere heart, with real intent, having faith in Christ, [*then*] he will manifest the truth of it unto you, by the power of the Holy Ghost."[5]

Even God's love, although infinite and perfect, is also subject to conditions.[6] For example:

"*If* ye keep my commandments, [*then*] ye shall abide in my love; even as I have kept my Father's commandments, and abide in his love."[7]

Elder D. Todd Christofferson further expounded on this gospel truth when he taught: "Some are wont to say, 'The Savior loves me just as I am,' and that is certainly true. But He cannot take any of us into His kingdom just as we are, 'for no unclean thing can dwell there, or dwell in his presence' [Moses 6:57]. Our sins must first be resolved."[8]

Weak Things Can Become Strong

The blessing of receiving God's power to help us change is also conditional. The Savior, speaking through the prophet Moroni in the Book of Mormon, taught: "If men come unto me I will show unto them their weakness. I give unto men weakness that they may be humble; and my grace is sufficient for all men that humble themselves before me; for if they humble themselves before me, and have faith in me, then will I make weak things become strong unto them."[9]

Looking more closely at what the Lord is teaching us here, we see that He first says that He gives men and women *weakness*, singular, which is part of our mortal experience as fallen or carnal beings. We have become natural men and women because of the Fall of Adam. But through the Atonement of Jesus Christ, we can overcome our weakness, or our fallen natures.

He then says that His grace is sufficient and that *if* we will humble ourselves and have faith in Him, *then* He will "make weak *things* [plural] become strong unto [us]." In other words, as we first change our fallen natures, our weakness, then we will be able to change our behaviors, our weaknesses.

Requirements of Change

Let's review the requirements to change according to the Lord's pattern:

First, we must humble ourselves. The Lord's condition for change is humility. "*If* they humble themselves before me,"[10] He said. The opposite of humility is pride. Pride exists when we think we know better—when what *we* think or feel takes priority over what *God* thinks or feels.

King Benjamin taught that "the natural man is an enemy to God, . . . and will be, forever and ever, unless he . . . putteth off the natural man and becometh a saint through the atonement of Christ the Lord, and becometh as a child, submissive, meek, [and] humble."[11]

In order to change, we need to put off the natural man and become humble and submissive. We must be humble enough to follow a living prophet. Humble enough to make and keep temple covenants. Humble enough to repent daily. We must be humble enough to want to change, to "yield our hearts unto God."[12]

Second, we must have faith in Jesus Christ. Again, the words of the Savior: "If they humble themselves before me, *and have faith in me*,"[13] He will give us the power to overcome our weaknesses. Humility, coupled with faith in Jesus Christ, will allow us to access the enabling power of His grace and the fulness of blessings available because of His Atonement.

President Nelson has taught that "true repentance begins with faith that Jesus Christ has the power to cleanse, heal, and strengthen us. . . . It is *our* faith that unlocks the power of God in *our* lives."[14]

Third, through His grace He can make weak things become strong. *If* we humble ourselves and have faith in Jesus Christ, *then*

His grace will enable us to change. In other words, He will empower us to change. This is possible because, as He says, "my grace is sufficient for all men."[15] His strengthening, enabling grace gives us power to overcome *all* obstacles, *all* challenges, and *all* weaknesses as we seek to change.

Our greatest weaknesses can become our greatest strengths. We can be changed and "become new creatures."[16] Weak things literally can "become strong unto [us]."[17]

The Savior worked out His infinite and eternal Atonement so that we could in fact change, repent, and become better. We can actually be born again. We can overcome habits, addictions, and even the "disposition to do evil."[18] As sons and daughters of a loving Father in Heaven, we have the power within us to change.

Examples of Change

The scriptures are full of examples of men and women who changed.

Saul, a Pharisee and active persecutor of the early Christian church,[19] became Paul, an Apostle of the Lord Jesus Christ.

Alma was a priest in the court of wicked King Noah. He heard the words of Abinadi, fully repented, and became one of the great missionaries of the Book of Mormon.

His son Alma spent his youth seeking to destroy the Church. He was among "the very vilest of sinners"[20] until he had a change of heart and became a powerful missionary in his own right.

Moses was adopted into Pharaoh's family and raised in luxury as an Egyptian prince. But when he came to understand who he really was and learned of his divine destiny, he changed and became the great lawgiving prophet of the Old Testament.[21]

My wife's grandfather James B. Keysor has always impressed me with his own mighty change of heart.[22] Born of faithful Latter-day Saint pioneer ancestors in the Salt Lake Valley in 1906, he lost his mother at a young age and struggled throughout his youth. His teenage and young adult years were spent away from the Church, during which time he acquired a number of bad habits. Nevertheless, he met and married a faithful woman, and together they raised five children.

In 1943, following the difficult years of the Great Depression and during World War II, Bud, as he was called by friends and family, left Utah and moved to Los Angeles, California, to look for employment. During this time away from home, he lived with his sister and her husband, who was serving as the bishop of their ward.

With the love and influence of his sister and brother-in-law, he started to revive his interest in the Church and began to read the Book of Mormon each night before going to sleep.

One night, while he was reading in Alma chapter 34, his heart was touched as he read the following words:

"Yea, I would that ye would come forth and harden not your hearts any longer. . . .

"For behold, this life is the time for men to prepare to meet God; yea, behold the day of this life is the day for men to perform their labors."[23]

While he was reading these verses, a powerful feeling came over him and he knew that he had to change, to repent, and he knew what he must do. He got up from his bed and knelt down and began to pray, pleading with the Lord to forgive him and to give him the strength he needed to make changes in his life. His prayer was answered, and from that time forward, he never looked back. Bud went on to serve in the Church and remained a faithful, committed Latter-day Saint to the end of his life. He was changed in every way. His mind, his heart, his actions, his very being were changed.

Brothers and sisters, our divine destiny and purpose is ultimately to become like our Heavenly Father and Savior, Jesus Christ. We do this as we change, or repent. We receive the Savior's "image in [our] countenances."[24] We become new, clean, different, and we simply continue to work at it every day. Sometimes it may feel like two steps forward and one step back, but we continue to humbly move forward in faith.

And as we humble ourselves and exercise faith in Jesus Christ, the grace of Christ and His infinite atoning sacrifice make it possible to change.

I witness and testify that Jesus Christ is in reality our Savior and Redeemer. His grace is indeed sufficient. I declare that He is "the way, the truth, and the life."[25] In the name of Jesus Christ, amen.

Notes

1. Thomas S. Monson, "See Others as They May Become," *Ensign* or *Liahona*, Nov. 2012, 69.
2. "The Family: A Proclamation to the World" states that "all human beings—male and female—are created in the image of God. Each is a beloved spirit son or daughter of heavenly parents, and, as such, each has a divine nature and destiny" (ChurchofJesusChrist.org).
3. Russell M. Nelson, "We Can Do Better and Be Better," *Ensign* or *Liahona*, May 2019, 67.
4. Doctrine and Covenants 14:7; emphasis added.
5. Moroni 10:4; emphasis added.
6. President Russell M. Nelson has taught: "While divine love can be called perfect, infinite, enduring, and universal, it cannot correctly be characterized as *unconditional*. The word does not appear in the scriptures. On the other hand, many verses affirm that the higher levels of love the Father and the Son feel for each of us—and certain divine blessings stemming from that love—are *conditional*" ("Divine Love," *Ensign*, Feb. 2003, 20–22; *Liahona*, Feb. 2003, 12–14).
7. John 15:10; emphasis added.
8. D. Todd Christofferson, "The Love of God," *Liahona*, Nov. 2021, 16.
9. Ether 12:27.
10. Ether 12:27; emphasis added.
11. Mosiah 3:19.
12. See Helaman 3:35.
13. Ether 12:27; emphasis added.
14. Russell M. Nelson, "Christ Is Risen; Faith in Him Will Move Mountains," *Liahona*, May 2021, 102.
15. Ether 12:27.
16. See Mosiah 27:24–26; see also 2 Corinthians 5:17.
17. Ether 12:27.
18. Mosiah 5:2.
19. See Acts 8:3; 26:10; Galatians 1:13; Philippians 3:6.
20. Mosiah 28:4.
21. See Doctrine and Covenants 138:41.
22. See Mosiah 5:2; Alma 5:14.
23. Alma 34:31–32.
24. Alma 5:14.
25. John 14:6.

CONVERSION TO THE WILL OF GOD

ELDER QUENTIN L. COOK
Of the Quorum of the Twelve Apostles

I am grateful for President Russell M. Nelson's powerful prophetic call to missionary service and President M. Russell Ballard's and Elder Marcos A. Aidukaitis's inspiring missionary messages today.

A missionary assignment to Great Britain late last year allowed me to reflect on the precious spiritual events that were foundational to my decision to serve as a missionary.[1] When I was 15 years old, my beloved older brother, Joe, was 20—the age of eligibility then to serve a mission. In the United States, because of the Korean conflict, very few were allowed to serve. Only one could be called from each ward per year.[2] It was a surprise when our bishop asked Joe to explore this possibility with our father. Joe had been preparing applications for medical school. Our father, who was not active in the Church, had made financial preparations to help him and was not in favor of Joe going on a mission. Dad suggested that Joe could do more good by going to medical school. This was a huge issue in our family.

In a remarkable discussion with my wise and exemplary older brother, we concluded that his decision on whether to serve a mission and delay his education depended on three questions: (1) Is Jesus Christ divine? (2) Is the Book of Mormon the word of God? and (3) Is Joseph Smith the Prophet of the Restoration? If the answer to these questions was yes, it was clear that Joe could do more good taking the gospel of Jesus Christ to the world than becoming a doctor at an earlier date.[3]

That night I prayed fervently and with real intent. The Spirit, in an undeniably powerful way, confirmed to me that the answer to all three of these questions was yes. This was a seminal event for me. I realized that every decision I would make for the rest of my life would be influenced by these truths. I also knew that I would serve a mission if given the opportunity. Over a lifetime of service and spiritual experiences, I have come to understand that true conversion is the result of the conscious acceptance of the will of God and that we can be guided in our actions by the Holy Ghost.

I already had a testimony of the divinity of Jesus Christ as Savior of the world. That night I received a spiritual testimony of the Book of Mormon[4] and the Prophet Joseph Smith.

Joseph Smith Was an Instrument in the Lord's Hands

Your testimony will be strengthened when you know in your heart through your prayers that the Prophet Joseph Smith was an instrument in the Lord's hands. During the past eight years, one of my assignments in the Twelve Apostles was to review and read all the remarkable Joseph Smith papers and documents and the research that led to the publication of the *Saints* volumes.[5] My testimony and admiration of the Prophet Joseph Smith have been greatly strengthened and enhanced after reading the inspiring details of his life and foreordained prophetic ministry.

Joseph's translation of the Book of Mormon by the gift and power of God was foundational to the Restoration.[6] The Book of Mormon is internally consistent, beautifully written, and contains the answers to life's great questions. It is another testament of Jesus Christ. I testify that Joseph Smith was righteous, full of faith, and an instrument in the Lord's hands in bringing forth the Book of Mormon.

The revelations and events recorded in the Doctrine and Covenants provide the keys, ordinances, and covenants necessary for salvation and exaltation. They not only set forth the essentials required to establish the Church but also provide profound doctrine that allows us to understand the purpose of life and gives us an eternal perspective.

One of the numerous examples of Joseph Smith's prophetic role is found in the 76th section of the Doctrine and Covenants. It is an explicit record of the vision of heaven, including kingdoms of glory, which the Prophet Joseph and Sidney Rigdon were blessed to receive on February 16, 1832. At that time, the vast majority of churches were teaching that the Savior's Atonement would not provide salvation for most people. It was believed that a few would be saved and the vast majority would be doomed to hell and damnation, including endless tortures "of the most awful and unspeakable intensity."[7]

The revelation contained in the 76th section provides a glorious vision of the degrees of glory where the vast majority of Heavenly Father's children who were valiant in their premortal estate are profoundly blessed following the ultimate judgment.[8] The vision of the three degrees of glory, the lowest of which "surpasses all understanding,"[9] is a direct refutation of the then strong but erroneous doctrine that the majority would be doomed to hell and damnation.

When you realize Joseph Smith was only 26 years old, had a limited education, and had little or no exposure to the classical languages from which the Bible was translated, he was truly an instrument in the Lord's hands. In the 17th verse of section 76, he was inspired to use the word *unjust* instead of *damnation* that was used in the Gospel of John.[10]

It is interesting that 45 years later an Anglican church leader and academically credentialed classical scholar,[11] Frederic W. Farrar, who wrote *The Life of Christ*,[12] asserted that the definition of *damnation* in the King James Version of the Bible was the result of translation errors from Hebrew and Greek to English.[13]

In our day, many have adopted the concept that there should be no consequence for sin. They support the unconditional condoning of sin without repentance. Our revealed doctrine not only refutes the idea that most people would be eternally condemned to hell and damnation but also establishes that personal repentance is a commanded prerequisite to partake of the Savior's Atonement and inherit the celestial kingdom.[14] I testify that Joseph Smith was truly an instrument in the Lord's hands in bringing forth the Restoration of His gospel!

Because of the Restoration of the gospel of Jesus Christ, we understand the importance of both repentance and the "works of righteousness."[15] We understand the overwhelming significance of the Savior's Atonement and of His saving ordinances and covenants, including those performed in the temple.

The "works of righteousness" emanate from and are the fruits of conversion. True conversion is brought about by the conscious acceptance and commitment to follow the will of God.[16] The banquet of consequences and blessings that flow from conversion is true and permanent peace and the personal assurance of ultimate happiness[17]—despite the storms of this life.

Conversion to the Savior changes a natural man into a sanctified, born again, purified person—a new creature in Christ Jesus.[18]

Many Are Kept from the Truth Because They Know Not Where to Find It

What are the obligations that flow from conversion? In Liberty Jail, the Prophet Joseph noted that many "are only kept from the truth because they know not where to find it."[19]

In the Lord's preface to the Doctrine and Covenants, a big-picture declaration of the Lord's purpose for us was set forth. He declared, "Wherefore, I the Lord, knowing the calamity which should come upon the inhabitants of the earth, called upon my servant Joseph Smith, Jun., and spake unto him from heaven, and gave him commandments." He further instructs, "That the fulness of my gospel might be proclaimed by the weak and the simple unto the ends of the world."[20] That includes full-time missionaries. That includes each of us. This should be a laser-like focus to everyone who has been blessed with a conversion to the will of God. The Savior graciously invites us to be His voice and His hands.[21] The love of the Savior will be our guiding light. The Savior taught His disciples, "Go ye therefore, and teach all nations."[22] And to Joseph Smith, He declared, "Preach my gospel unto every creature who has not received it."[23]

One week after the dedication of the Kirtland Temple on April 3, 1836, which was Easter Sunday and also Passover, the Lord appeared in a magnificent vision to Joseph and Oliver Cowdery. The Lord accepted the temple and declared, "This is the beginning of the blessing which shall be poured out upon the heads of my people."[24]

After this vision closed, Moses appeared "and committed . . . the keys of the gathering of Israel from the four parts of the earth, and the leading of the ten tribes from the land of the north."[25]

President Russell M. Nelson, our beloved prophet today who holds these same keys, taught this morning: "You young men have been reserved for this time when the promised gathering of Israel is taking place. As you serve missions, you play a pivotal role in this unprecedented event!"[26]

For the Savior's mandate to share the gospel to become part of who we are, we need to become **converted** to the will of God; we need to **love** our neighbors, **share** the restored gospel of Jesus Christ, and **invite** all to come and see. As members of the Church, we cherish the Prophet Joseph's reply to John Wentworth, the editor of the *Chicago Democrat*, in 1842. He was requesting information about the Church. Joseph concluded his response by using the "Standard of Truth" as a preface to the thirteen Articles of Faith. The standard conveys, in a concise way, what must be accomplished:

"No unhallowed hand can stop the work from progressing; persecutions may rage, mobs may combine, armies may assemble, calumny may defame, but the truth of God will go forth boldly, nobly, and independent, till it has penetrated every continent, visited every clime, swept every country, and sounded in every ear, till the purposes of God shall be accomplished, and the Great Jehovah shall say the work is done."[27]

This has been the clarion call for generations of Latter-day Saints, especially missionaries. In the spirit of the "Standard of Truth," we are grateful that in the midst of a worldwide pandemic, faithful missionaries have shared the gospel. Missionaries, we love you! The Lord asks each one of us to share His gospel in word and deed. Our personal conversion includes the responsibility to share the gospel of Jesus Christ with the world.

The blessings of sharing the gospel include increasing our conversion to the will of God and letting God prevail in our lives.[28] We bless others to experience a "mighty change" of heart.[29] There is truly eternal joy in helping to bring souls unto Christ.[30] Laboring for the conversion of oneself and others is *the* noble task.[31] I so testify in the name of Jesus Christ, amen.

Notes

1. I served in the British Mission from September 1, 1960, to September 1, 1962.
2. The other young men had to be available for the military draft.
3. After Joe's return from his mission, he did graduate from medical school and serve as a successful doctor. His mission also prepared him to be a bishop, stake president, regional representative, and mission president.
4. See Moroni 10:4. I had already read the Book of Mormon. With the seriousness of this issue in our family, I was praying with real intent.
5. See *Saints: The Story of the Church of Jesus Christ in the Latter Days*, vol. 1, *The Standard of Truth, 1815–1846* (2018), and vol. 2, *No Unhallowed Hand, 1846–1893* (2020).
6. The translation commenced on April 7, 1829, and was completed around the first of July 1829. It has been remarkable to study the facts surrounding the translation. I particularly appreciated reading the printer's manuscript and the original manuscript of the Book of Mormon published as volumes 3 and 5 in the Revelations and Translations series of *The Joseph Smith Papers*. They are both landmark volumes.
7. Frederic W. Farrar, *Eternal Hope: Five Sermons Preached in Westminster Abbey, November and December, 1877* (1892), xxii.
8. The vision includes those who do not learn of Christ in this life, children who die before the age of accountability, and those who have no understanding.
9. Doctrine and Covenants 76:89.
10. See John 5:29.
11. Farrar was educated at King's College, London, and Trinity College, Cambridge. He was a Church of England (Anglican) cleric, archdeacon of Westminster Abbey, dean of Canterbury Cathedral, and chaplain to the Royal Household.
12. See Frederic W. Farrar, *The Life of Christ* (1874).
13. See Farrar, *Eternal Hope*, xxxvi–xxxvii. Frederic Farrar felt compelled to correct teachings about damnation and hell. He strongly proclaimed what he termed "simple, undeniable, and indisputable facts. . . . The verb 'to damn' and its cognates does not once occur in the Old Testament. No word conveying any such meaning occurs in the Greek of the New Testament." He goes on to explain that the word *damnation* is a "grievous mistranslation . . . [and] perverts and obscures the real meaning of our Lord's utterances" (*Eternal Hope*, xxxvii). Farrar also pointed out the overwhelming demonstration of a loving Father in Heaven throughout the Bible as additional evidence that the definitions of *hell* and *damnation* used in the English translation were incorrect (see *Eternal Hope*, xiv–xv, xxxiv, 93; see also Quentin L. Cook, "Our Father's Plan—Big Enough for All His Children," *Ensign* or *Liahona*, May 2009, 36).
14. The relationship between repentance and the Atonement is set forth in Doctrine and Covenants 19:15–18, 20. In addition, endless punishment is clarified in Doctrine and Covenants 19:10–12.
15. Doctrine and Covenants 59:23.
16. See Mosiah 27:25; Doctrine and Covenants 112:13; see also Dale E. Miller, "Bringing Peace and Healing to Your Soul," *Ensign* or *Liahona*, Nov. 2004, 12–14.
17. See Mosiah 2:41.
18. See Dallin H. Oaks, "The Challenge to Become," *Ensign*, Nov. 2000, 33; *Liahona*, Jan. 2001, 41; see also 2 Corinthians 5:17; Bible Dictionary, "Conversion."
19. Doctrine and Covenants 123:12.
20. Doctrine and Covenants 1:17, 23.
21. If that is our desire, we are "called to the work" (Doctrine and Covenants 4:3; see also Thomas S. Monson, "Called to the Work," *Ensign* or *Liahona*, June 2017, 4–5).
22. Matthew 28:19.
23. Doctrine and Covenants 112:28.

24. Doctrine and Covenants 110:10.
25. Doctrine and Covenants 110:11.
26. See Russell M. Nelson, "Preaching the Gospel of Peace," *Liahona*, May 2022, 6–7; see also Russell M. Nelson, "Hope of Israel" (worldwide youth devotional, June 3, 2018), HopeofIsrael.ChurchofJesusChrist.org.
27. *Teachings of Presidents of the Church: Joseph Smith* (2007), 444.
28. See Russell M. Nelson, "Let God Prevail," *Ensign* or *Liahona*, Nov. 2020, 92–95.
29. Alma 5:14.
30. See Doctrine and Covenants 18:15; see also James 5:19–20.
31. See Alma 26:22; Doctrine and Covenants 18:13–16; see also Bible Dictionary, "Conversion."

WOMEN'S SESSION

———

APRIL 2, 2022

INTRODUCTORY MESSAGE

PRESIDENT DALLIN H. OAKS
First Counselor in the First Presidency

My dear sisters, as we begin this unique women's session of general conference, I am pleased to deliver this introductory message from the First Presidency.

Our Saturday sessions have a history of different purposes and different audiences. This evening we add to that history as we embark upon a new purpose and procedure for the foreseeable future. The gospel of Jesus Christ does not change. Gospel doctrine does not change. Our personal covenants do not change. But over the years, the meetings we hold to communicate our messages do change and very likely will continue to change over the years.

For now, this Saturday evening meeting is a session of general conference, not a session of any organization. Like all sessions of general conference, the planning, speakers, and music are designated by the First Presidency.

We have asked President Jean B. Bingham, General President of the Relief Society, to conduct this session. Future Saturday evening sessions may be conducted by one of the other General Officers of the Church, such as members of the General Presidencies of Relief Society, Young Women, and Primary, designated by the First Presidency.

Tonight this Saturday evening session of general conference will concentrate on the concerns of Latter-day Saint women. This will include the doctrine of The Church of Jesus Christ of Latter-day Saints, the policies of the Church that relate specially to women, and the general responsibilities and work of the organizations that include the women and girls of the Church. Though this session is deliberately broadcast to a worldwide audience like all sessions of general conference, the audience invited to be present in the Conference Center for this session is women and girls age 12 and older. We have included some priesthood leaders who preside over the participating organizations.

What we are initiating here is responsive to the communication resources currently available to the Lord's worldwide Church leadership and membership. The doctrine of the gospel of Jesus Christ is for everyone, so that is our principal motive and extent of dissemination. We honor the daughters of God in this special session by concentrating on their concerns and those of their organizations.

We are grateful that broadcast technology now gives Church leaders the capacity to conduct detailed training by addressing specific audiences in the field. We also welcome the fact that current travel opportunities are increasing. That allows us to send Church leaders to conduct needed regular face-to-face leadership training in the field.

This is the work of the Lord Jesus Christ. We are His servants, directed by His Holy Spirit. We invoke the blessings of our Lord upon the leaders of these organizations and upon the faithful women and girls who serve the Lord in these organizations and in their individual lives. In the name of Jesus Christ, amen.

LESSONS AT THE WELL

SUSAN H. PORTER
First Counselor in the Primary General Presidency

What a joy it is to be gathered with each of you in this women's session of general conference!

I grew up in western New York and attended a small branch of the Church about 20 miles (32 km) from our home. As I sat in Sunday School class in the basement of our old rented chapel with only my friend Patti Jo, I never could have imagined being part of a global sisterhood of millions of women.

Five years ago my husband, Bruce, became seriously ill when we were serving with the consecrated Saints in the Europe East Area. We returned home, and he passed away only a few weeks later. My life changed overnight. I was grieving and felt weak and vulnerable. I pled with the Lord to direct my path: "What would Thou have me do?"

A few weeks later, I was going through my mail when a small picture in a catalog caught my eye. As I looked closer, I realized it was an artist's rendition of the Samaritan woman with Jesus at the well. At that moment the Spirit spoke clearly to me: "*That* is what you are supposed to do." A loving Heavenly Father was inviting me to come to the Savior and learn.

I would like to share with you three lessons I am learning as I continue to drink from His well of "living water."[1]

First: Our Past and Present Circumstances Do Not Determine Our Future

Sisters, I know that many of you feel as I did, unsure how to face difficult challenges and loss—loss because your life is not unfolding in the way you had hoped for, prayed for, and planned for.

No matter our circumstances, our lives are sacred and have meaning and purpose. Each of us is a beloved daughter of God, born with divinity in our souls.

Our Savior, Jesus Christ, through His atoning sacrifice, made it possible for us to be cleansed and healed, enabling us to fulfill our purpose on earth regardless of decisions of family members, our marital status, physical or mental health, or any other situation.

Consider the woman at the well. What was her life like? Jesus perceived that she had had five husbands and was currently not married to the man she was living with. And yet, despite her life's difficulties, one of the Savior's first public declarations that He was the Messiah was to her. He said, "I that speak unto thee am he."[2]

She became a powerful witness, declaring to those in her city that Jesus was the Christ. "And many of the Samaritans of that city believed on him for the saying of the woman."[3]

Her past and present circumstances did not determine her future. Like her, we can choose to turn to the Savior today for the strength and healing that will enable us to fulfill *all* that we were sent here to do.

Second: The Power Is in Us

In a familiar verse in the Doctrine and Covenants, the Lord encourages women and men to be "anxiously engaged in a good cause, and do many things of their own free will, and bring to pass much righteousness; *for the power is in them.*"[4]

Sisters, the power is in *us* to bring to pass much righteousness!

President Russell M. Nelson testified, "Every woman and every man who makes covenants with God and keeps those covenants, and who participates worthily in priesthood ordinances, has direct access to the power of God."[5]

I have come to know that as we strive to honor sacred covenants made at baptism and in holy temples, the Lord will bless us "with *His* healing, strengthening power" and with "spiritual insights and awakenings [we've] never had before."[6]

Third: "Out of Small Things Proceedeth That Which Is Great"[7]

In the Sermon on the Mount, Jesus taught His disciples, "Ye are the *salt* of the earth"[8] and "Ye are the *light* of the world."[9] Later He compared the growth of the kingdom of heaven to leaven, "which a woman took, and hid in three measures of meal, till the whole was leavened."[10]

- Salt
- Leaven
- Light

Even in very small amounts, each affects everything around it. The Savior invites us to use His power to be as *salt*, *leaven*, and *light*.

Salt

It is surprising how much difference a sprinkling of salt makes in the flavor of what we eat. And yet salt is one of the least expensive and simplest ingredients.

In the book of 2 Kings, we read of "a little maid"[11] who was captured by the Syrians and became a servant to the wife of Naaman, captain of the Syrian army. She was *as salt*; she was young, of no worldly importance, and her life as a slave in a foreign country was clearly not what she had hoped for.

However, she spoke two sentences with the power of God, testifying to Naaman's wife: "Would God my lord were with the prophet that is in Samaria! for he would recover him of his leprosy."[12]

Her words of faith were relayed to Naaman, who acted on her words, allowing him to be healed both physically and spiritually.

We often focus on the servants who convinced Naaman to bathe in the river Jordan, as the prophet Elisha directed, but Naaman would not have even been at Elisha's door without "a little maid."

You may be young or feel of no importance, but you can be *as salt* in your family, at school, and in your community.

Leaven

Have you ever eaten bread without leaven? How would you describe it? Dense? Heavy? Hard? With only a small amount of leaven, bread rises, expanding to become lighter and softer.

When we invite the power of God into our lives, we can replace the "spirit of heaviness"[13] with inspired perspectives that lift others and make room for hearts to be healed.

Recently a friend of mine lay in bed on Christmas morning, overcome with sorrow. Her children begged her to get up; however, she was filled with the pain of her pending divorce. Lying in bed sobbing, she poured out her soul in prayer to her Heavenly Father, telling Him of her despair.

As she concluded her prayer, the Spirit whispered to her that God knew her pain. She was filled with His compassion for her. This sacred experience validated her emotions and gave her hope that she was not grieving alone. She got up, went outside, and built a snowman with her children, replacing the heaviness of the morning with laughter and joy.

Light

How much light does it take to pierce the darkness in a room? One small ray. And that ray of light in a dark place can emanate from the power of God in you.

Even though you may feel alone as the storms of life are raging, you can shine a light in the darkness of misunderstanding, confusion, and unbelief. Your light of faith in Christ can be steady and sure, leading those around you to safety and peace.

Sisters, hearts can be changed and lives blessed as we offer a pinch of salt, a spoonful of leaven, and a ray of light.

I testify that the *Savior* is the salt in our lives, inviting *us* to taste of His joy and love.[14] It is *He* who is the leaven when our lives are hard, bringing *us* hope[15] and lifting our burdens[16] through His matchless power and redeeming love.[17] *He* is our light,[18] illuminating *our* path back home.

I pray that we can come to the Savior, like the woman at the well, and drink of His living water. With the people of Samaria, we can then declare, "Now we believe, . . . for we have heard him ourselves, and know that this is indeed the Christ, the Saviour of the world."[19] In the name of Jesus Christ, amen.

Notes

1. John 4:10.
2. John 4:26.
3. John 4:39.

4. Doctrine and Covenants 58:27–28; emphasis added.
5. Russell M. Nelson, "Spiritual Treasures," *Ensign* or *Liahona*, Nov. 2019, 77. "Every time you worthily serve and worship in the temple, you leave armed with God's power and with His angels having 'charge over' you [Doctrine and Covenants 109:22]."
6. Russell M. Nelson, "The Temple and Your Spiritual Foundation," *Liahona*, Nov. 2021, 94, 95.
7. Doctrine and Covenants 64:33.
8. Matthew 5:13; emphasis added.
9. Matthew 5:14; emphasis added.
10. Matthew 13:33.
11. 2 Kings 5:2.
12. 2 Kings 5:3.
13. Isaiah 61:3.
14. See Alma 36:24–25.
15. See Ether 12:4.
16. See Matthew 11:28–30.
17. See Alma 5:9.
18. See Psalm 27:1; John 8:12; Doctrine and Covenants 88:50; see also Sharon Eubank, "Christ: The Light That Shines in Darkness," *Ensign* or *Liahona*, May 2019, 73–76.
19. John 4:42.

DO WHAT MATTERETH MOST

REBECCA L. CRAVEN

Second Counselor in the Young Women General Presidency

Not long ago, a dear friend had an impression to visit a woman in her ward. She brushed off the prompting because she hardly knew her—it just didn't make sense. But since the thought kept coming to her, she decided to act on the prompting. Because she was already feeling uncomfortable about the impending visit, she determined that taking something to the sister would help ease her anxiety. Certainly she couldn't go empty-handed! So she bought a container of ice cream, and off she went to begin what she worried might be an awkward visit.

She knocked on the woman's door, and shortly the sister answered. My friend handed her the ice cream in a brown paper bag, and the conversation began. It didn't take long for my friend to realize why the visit was needed. As they sat together on the front porch, the woman unveiled a host of challenges she was facing. After an hour of talking in the warm summer weather, my friend noticed the ice cream melting through the brown paper bag.

She exclaimed, "I am so sorry that your ice cream melted!"

The woman sweetly responded, "It's OK! I'm lactose intolerant!"

In a dream, the Lord told the prophet Lehi, "Blessed art thou Lehi, because of the things which thou hast *done*."[1]

Being a disciple of Jesus Christ involves more than just hoping or believing. It calls for effort, movement, and commitment. It requires that we do something, being "doers of the word, and not hearers only."[2]

In the case of the melted ice cream, what mattered most? The ice cream? Or that my friend simply did something?

I had a sweet experience with a darling young woman who asked a very sincere question: "Sister Craven, how do you know that anything about the Church is true? Because I feel nothing."

Before jumping to an answer, I first asked her some questions. "Tell me about your personal scripture study."

"Bendito eres tú, Lehi, por lo que has hecho."

"hacedores de la palabra, y no tan solamente oidores."

She replied, "I don't read the scriptures."

I asked, "What about with your family? Do you study *Come, Follow Me* together?"

She said, "No."

I asked about her prayers: "What do you feel when you pray?"

Her answer: "I don't pray."

My response to her was simple: "If you want to know anything, you will have to do something."

Isn't that true with anything we want to learn or know? I invited my new friend to start *doing* the gospel of Jesus Christ: praying, studying, serving others, and trusting in the Lord. Conversion won't come while doing nothing. It comes through the power of the Holy Ghost as we intentionally make an effort to know by asking, seeking, and knocking. It comes by doing.[3]

In the Doctrine and Covenants, the Lord occasionally says, "It mattereth not."[4] It makes me ponder that if some things matter not, or matter less, there must be things that matter most. In our efforts to *do something* or *do anything*, we might ask ourselves, "What mattereth most?"

Advertisers often use slogans such as "Essential" or "Must Have" in the hope of luring us to believe the product they are selling is necessary for our happiness or well-being. But is what they are selling *really* essential? Must we *really* have it? Does it *really* matter?

Here are some thoughts to consider. What mattereth most?

- How many "likes" we get on our social media posts? Or how much we are loved and valued by our Heavenly Father?
- Wearing the latest trend in clothing? Or showing respect for our bodies by dressing modestly?
- Finding answers through an internet search? Or receiving answers from God through the Holy Ghost?
- Wanting more? Or being content with what we have been given?

President Russell M. Nelson teaches:

"With the Holy Ghost as your companion, you can see right through the celebrity culture that has smitten our society. You can be smarter than previous generations have ever been. . . .

"Set a standard for the rest of the world!"[5]

It takes effort to stay focused on what is *truly essential* for lasting joy. Satan would love nothing more than for us to misplace our eternal values, leading us to waste precious time, talents, or spiritual strength on things that matter not. I invite each of us to prayerfully consider those things that distract us from doing what mattereth most.

Our oldest son's third-grade teacher taught her class to "boss your brain." It was a reminder to her young students that they were in control of their thoughts and could therefore control what they do. I remind myself to "boss *my* brain" when I find myself drifting toward things that matter less.

A high school student recently told me that it has become popular among some youth of the Church to disregard the commandments with a calculated plan to repent later. "It's sort of a badge of honor," I was told. Certainly the Lord will continue to forgive those who humbly repent "with real intent."[6] But the Savior's merciful Atonement should never be used in such a mocking way. We know the parable of the one lost sheep. Of course, a shepherd will leave the other 99 sheep to find the one who has strayed. But can you imagine the joy that those who choose to be the 99 bring to the Good Shepherd? The ones who stick together and help each other live their covenants? Can you visualize what the world or your school or your work or your home would be like if being obedient was the popular thing to do? It's not about *doing* life perfectly—it's about finding joy while *doing our best* to live the covenants we have made with the Lord.

With the world expressing more doubt about God and confusion and pressures increasing, this is the time we must stay closest to the prophet. As he is the Lord's mouthpiece, we can trust that what he urges, counsels, and pleads with us to do are things that matter most.

Although it may not be easy, there is always a way to do the right thing. While talking with a group of friends at school, a young woman felt her heart drop when the conversation turned to criticizing the standards of the Church. She realized she couldn't stay silent—she had to do something. Respectfully, she spoke of the love of Heavenly Father and how the commandments He set are to bless and protect His children. It would have been much easier for her to do nothing. But what mattered most? Blending in with the crowd? Or standing *out* as a witness of God at "all times and in all things, and in all places"?[7]

If the restored Church of Jesus Christ is going to come out of obscurity, we must come out of obscurity. As covenant-keeping women, we must shine our gospel light all over the world by stepping up and standing out. We do this together as daughters of God—a force of 8.2 million women ages 11 and beyond, whose work is exactly the same. We are gathering Israel as we participate in the work of salvation and exaltation: striving to live the gospel of Jesus Christ, caring for others in need, inviting all to receive the gospel, and uniting families for eternity.[8] The gospel of Jesus Christ is a gospel of action and a gospel of joy! Let us not underestimate our capacity to do those things that matter most. Our divine heritage gives us courage and confidence to do and be all that our loving Heavenly Father knows we can be.

The youth theme for this year is from Proverbs 3:5–6:

"Trust in the Lord with all thine heart; and lean not unto thine own understanding.

"In all thy ways acknowledge him, and he shall direct thy paths."

A key component of trusting in the Lord is moving forward, believing He will guide us even when we don't have all the answers.

Sisters, it's not about the ice cream. And it's not about doing more. It's about doing what matters. It's applying the doctrine of Christ in our lives as we strive to become more like Him.

The more we do to stay firmly on the covenant path, the more our faith in Jesus Christ will grow. The more our faith grows, the more we will desire to repent. And the more we repent, the more we will strengthen our covenant relationship with God. That covenant relationship draws us to the temple because keeping temple covenants is how we endure to the end.

As we center our lives on Jesus Christ, we will be guided to do what mattereth most. And we will be blessed with spiritual strength, contentment, and with *joy*! In the name of Jesus Christ, amen.

Notes

1. 1 Nephi 2:1; emphasis added.
2. James 1:22.
3. See Alma 5:45–46; Russell M. Nelson, "Drawing the Power of Jesus Christ into Our Lives," *Ensign* or *Liahona*, May 2017, 39–42.
4. See Doctrine and Covenants 27:2; 80:3.
5. Russell M. Nelson, "Hope of Israel" (worldwide youth devotional, June 3, 2018), HopeofIsrael.ChurchofJesusChrist.org.
6. Moroni 6:8.
7. Mosiah 18:9; see also "Young Women Theme," ChurchofJesusChrist.org.
8. See *General Handbook: Serving in The Church of Jesus Christ of Latter-day Saints*, 1.2, ChurchofJesusChrist.org.

COVENANTS WITH GOD STRENGTHEN, PROTECT, AND PREPARE US FOR ETERNAL GLORY

JEAN B. BINGHAM
Relief Society General President

Sisters, what a joy to gather in a worldwide sisterhood! As women who make and keep covenants with God, we share spiritual bonds that help us meet the challenges of our day and prepare us for the Second Coming of Jesus Christ. And keeping those covenants allows us to be women of influence who can draw others to the Savior.

Those who have been baptized covenanted on that never-to-be-forgotten day to take Jesus Christ's name upon them, to always remember Him, to keep His commandments, and to serve Him to the end. When we do these things, Heavenly Father promises to forgive our sins and give us the companionship of the Holy Ghost. These blessings start us on the path that, if we press forward and endure to the end, will allow us to live with Him and His Son in the celestial kingdom. *Every* baptized person has the promise of these privileges if she or he keeps the covenant made that special day.

Those who make further covenants in the temple receive powerful promises conditioned on personal faithfulness. We solemnly promise to obey God's commandments, live the gospel of Jesus Christ, be morally pure, and dedicate our time and talents to the Lord. In return, God promises blessings in this life and the opportunity to return to Him.[1] In that process, we are given, or endowed with, the power to discern between truth and error, between right and wrong, amid the confusing and negative voices that bombard us. What a powerful gift!

In preparation for my first trip to the temple, my mother and experienced Relief Society sisters helped me select the items I would need, including beautiful ceremonial clothing. But the most important preparation came even before knowing what to wear. After interviewing me to determine if I was worthy, my bishop explained the covenants I would make. His careful explanation gave me the chance to think about and be prepared to make those covenants.

When the day came, I participated with a feeling of gratitude and peace. Even though I did not understand the full significance of the covenants I made, I did know that I was bound to God through those covenants and was promised blessings I could scarcely comprehend if I kept them. Since that first experience, I have been continually assured that keeping the covenants we make with God allows us to draw upon the Savior's power, which strengthens us in our inevitable trials, provides protection from the adversary's influence, and prepares us for eternal glory.

Life's experiences can range from humorous to heart-wrenching, from grim to glorious. Each experience helps us understand more about our Father's encompassing love and our capacity to change through the Savior's gift of grace. Keeping our covenants allows the Savior's power to cleanse us as we learn through experience—whether it is a minor misjudgment or a major failing. Our Redeemer is there to catch us when we fall *if* we turn to Him.

Have you ever stood on a high cliff with your toes on its edge and your back to the abyss below? In rappelling, even though you are securely connected to a system of strong ropes and equipment that can deliver you to safety, standing on the edge is still heart-racing. Stepping backward off the cliff and swinging into thin air requires trust in an anchor secured to an immovable object. It demands trust in the person who will apply tension to the rope as you descend. And although the equipment provides you with some ability to control your descent, you must have confidence that your partner will not allow you to fall.

I vividly remember rappelling with a group of young women. I was first in the group to go. As I stepped backwards off the cliff, I began to fall without control. Gratefully, the rope jerked and my too-rapid descent was stopped. As I dangled halfway down the jagged rock face, I prayed fervently for whomever or whatever was keeping me from dropping onto the rocks.

Later, I learned that the anchor bolt had not been securely set, and as I stepped off the edge, the person belaying me was jerked on his back and pulled towards the edge of the cliff. Somehow, he wedged his feet against some rocks. Stabilized in that position, he was able to laboriously lower me, hand over hand, with the rope. Although I couldn't see him, I knew he was working with all his strength to save me. Another friend was at the bottom of the cliff, prepared to catch me if the rope ceased to hold. As I came within reach, he caught my harness and lowered me to the ground.

With Jesus Christ as our anchor and perfect partner, we are assured of His loving strength in trial and of eventual deliverance through Him. As President M. Russell Ballard taught: "Faith in God and in his Son, the Lord Jesus Christ, is the . . . anchor we must have in our lives to hold us fast during times of social turbulence and wickedness. . . . Our faith . . . must be centered in Jesus Christ, his life and his atonement, and in the restoration of his gospel."[2]

The spiritual equipment that keeps us from being broken on the rocks of adversity is our testimony of Jesus Christ and the covenants we make. We can rely on these supports to guide and carry us to safety. As our willing partner, the Savior will not allow us to fall beyond His reach. Even in our times of suffering and sorrow, He is there to lift and encourage. His power helps us recover from the often-devastating impact of others' choices. However, we each must put on the harness and make sure the knots are securely tied. We must choose to be anchored to the Savior, to be bound to Him by our covenants.[3]

How do we strengthen that anchor? We pray with a humble heart, study and ponder the scriptures, take the sacrament with a spirit of repentance and reverence, strive to keep the commandments, and follow the prophet's counsel. And as we fulfill our everyday tasks in "higher and holier"[4] ways, we become more connected to the Savior and, at the same time, help others come unto Him.

What does that "higher and holier" way look like? We try to live the gospel in all our interactions. We care for those in need by truly ministering, expressing love through simple service. We share the good news of the gospel with those who need peace and strength and "know not where to find it."⁵ We work to unite families for eternity on both sides of the veil. And for those who have made covenants in the house of the Lord, as President Russell M. Nelson explained, "Each adult temple patron will wear the sacred garment of the priesthood, [which] . . . reminds us . . . to walk on the covenant path each day in a higher and holier way."⁶ These actions are not just an occasional splurge but are essential to our daily happiness—and eternal joy.

There is nothing more important to our eternal progress than keeping our covenants with God. When our temple covenants are in force, we can trust in a joyful reunion with loved ones on the other side of the veil. That child or parent or spouse who has left mortality is hoping with all his or her heart that you will be true to the covenants that bind you together. If we disregard or treat lightly our covenants with God, we are putting those eternal ties in danger. Now is the time to repent, repair, and try again.

Happiness is hollow if we exchange the blessings of eternal joy for momentary ease. No matter our age, that is the absolute truth: the key to lasting happiness is living the gospel of Jesus Christ and keeping our covenants. Our prophet, President Nelson, has affirmed that "our ultimate security and our only enduring happiness lies in holding to the iron rod of the restored gospel of Jesus Christ, complete with its covenants and ordinances. When we do so, we can safely navigate through rough waters because we have access to God's power."⁷

Many of us are experiencing rough waters. As we are tossed by waves of adversity and are sometimes blinded by the torrents of tears that come in those difficulties, we may not know which direction to paddle our life's boat. We may not even think we have the strength to get to shore. Remembering *who* you are—a beloved child of God—*why* you are on the earth, and your *goal* of living with God and your loved ones can clear your vision and point you in the right direction. In the midst of the storm, there is a bright light to show the way. "I am the light which shineth in darkness," Jesus declared.⁸

We are assured of safety when we look to His light and maintain the integrity of our covenants.

It has been a privilege to meet women of all ages living in a wide variety of circumstances who are keeping their covenants. Each day, they look to the Lord and His prophet for guidance, rather than to popular media. Despite their individual challenges and the detrimental philosophies of the world that try to dissuade them from keeping their covenants, they are determined to stay on the covenant path. They rely on the promise of "all that [the] Father hath."[9] And whatever your age, each of you women who has made covenants with God has the ability to hold up the Lord's light and lead others to Him.[10] Through your keeping of covenants, He will bless you with His priesthood power and enable you to have a profound influence on all with whom you interact. As President Nelson declared, you are the women who will fulfill the prophecies that have been foretold![11]

Dear sisters, above all else, stay on the covenant path to Jesus Christ! We have been blessed to come to earth when temples dot the globe. Making and keeping temple covenants is available to every worthy member of the Church. Young adults, you don't need to wait until marriage or a mission to make those sacred covenants. You can prepare as a young woman to receive the protection and strength temple covenants give as soon after the age of 18 as you are ready and feel a desire to honor those temple covenants.[12] You who have already received the blessings of the temple, don't let detractors or distractions pull you away from eternal truths. Study and ask trusted sources for greater understanding of the sacred significance of the covenants you have made. Go to the temple as often as you can and listen to the Spirit. You will feel sweet reassurance that you are on the Lord's path. You will find the courage to continue as well as to bring others with you.

I testify that as we choose to make covenants with Heavenly Father and access the power of the Savior to keep them, we will be blessed with more happiness in this life than we can now imagine and a glorious eternal life to come.[13] In the name of Jesus Christ, amen.

Notes

1. See "About the Temple Endowment," temples.ChurchofJesusChrist.org.
2. M. Russell Ballard, "Anchor Your Soul," *New Era*, Mar. 1993, 4.
3. See Matthew 11:28–30.
4. See Marianne Holman Prescott, "The Higher and Holier Way," *Church News*, May 8, 2019, 18.
5. Doctrine and Covenants 123:12.
6. Russell M. Nelson, "Closing Remarks," *Ensign* or *Liahona*, Nov. 2019, 121.
7. Russell M. Nelson, in Sarah Jane Weaver, "Prophet Addresses 49,089 in Seattle's Safeco Field," *Church News*, Sept. 23, 2018, 8.
8. Doctrine and Covenants 6:21.
9. Doctrine and Covenants 84:38.
10. See 3 Nephi 18:24.
11. See Russell M. Nelson, "A Plea to My Sisters," *Ensign* or *Liahona*, Nov. 2015, 96.
12. See *General Handbook: Serving in The Church of Jesus Christ of Latter-day Saints*, 26.5.1, ChurchofJesusChrist.org.
13. See "The Living Christ: The Testimony of the Apostles," ChurchofJesusChrist.org.

YOUR DIVINE NATURE AND ETERNAL DESTINY

ELDER DALE G. RENLUND
Of the Quorum of the Twelve Apostles

Dear sisters, thank you for being here. I am honored to participate in this women's session of general conference. On occasion I have also been privileged to attend Young Women classes. But let me point out the obvious—I am not young, and I am not a woman! I learned, however, that I feel less out of place if I can recite the Young Women theme along with the young women. The profound doctrine taught in the Young Women theme[1] is important for young women, but it is applicable to all, including those of us who are not young women.

The Young Women theme begins, "I am a beloved daughter of heavenly parents, with a divine nature and eternal destiny."[2] This statement contains four important truths. First, you are a beloved daughter. Nothing you do—or do not do—can change that. God loves you because you are His spirit daughter. Sometimes we may not feel His love, but it is always there. God's love is perfect.[3] Our ability to sense that love is not.

The Spirit plays a pivotal role in communicating God's love to us.[4] Yet the influence of the Holy Ghost can be obscured "by strong emotions, such as anger, hate, . . . [or] fear, . . . like trying to savor the delicate flavor of a grape while eating a jalapeño pepper. . . . [One flavor] completely overpowers the other."[5] So too, behaviors that distance us from the Holy Ghost, including sin,[6] make it difficult for us to perceive God's love for us.

Similarly, our sense of God's love may be blunted by challenging circumstances and physical or mental illness, among other things. In all these cases, the counsel of trusted leaders or professionals can often be beneficial. We can also try to improve our receptivity to God's love by asking ourselves, "Is my love for God constant, or do I love Him when I have good days but not so much when I have bad days?"

The second truth is that we have heavenly parents, a father and a mother.[7] The doctrine of a Heavenly Mother comes by revelation and is a distinctive belief among Latter-day Saints. President Dallin H. Oaks explained the importance of this truth: "Our theology begins with heavenly parents. Our highest aspiration is to be like them."[8]

Very little has been revealed about Mother in Heaven, but what we do know is summarized in a gospel topic found in our Gospel Library application.[9] Once you have read what is there, you will know everything that I know about the subject. I wish I knew more. You too may still have questions and want to find more answers. Seeking greater understanding is an important part of our spiritual development, but please be cautious. Reason cannot replace revelation.

Speculation will not lead to greater spiritual knowledge, but it can lead us to deception or divert our focus from what has been revealed.[10] For example, the Savior taught His disciples, "Always pray unto the Father in my name."[11] We follow this pattern and direct our worship to our Heavenly Father in the name of Jesus Christ and do not pray to Heavenly Mother.[12]

Ever since God appointed prophets, they have been authorized to speak on His behalf. But they do not pronounce doctrines fabricated "of [their] own mind"[13] or teach what has not been revealed. Consider the words of the Old Testament prophet Balaam, who was offered a bribe to curse the Israelites to benefit Moab. Balaam said, "If [the king of Moab] would give me his house full of silver and gold, I cannot go beyond the word of the Lord my God, to do less or more."[14] Latter-day prophets are similarly constrained. Demanding revelation from God is both arrogant and unproductive. Instead, we wait on the Lord and His timetable to reveal His truths through the means that He has established.[15]

The third truth in the opening paragraph of the Young Women theme is that we have "a divine nature." This is intrinsic to who we are. It is spiritually "genetic," inherited from our heavenly parents,[16] and requires no effort on our part. This is our most important identity, regardless of how else we choose to identify ourselves. Understanding this profound truth is important for everyone but especially for individuals belonging to groups who have been historically marginalized, oppressed, or subjugated. Remember that your most important identity relates to your divine nature as a child of God.

The fourth truth is that we have an "eternal destiny." Such a destiny will not be forced on us. After death, we will receive what we have qualified for and "enjoy [only] that which [we] are willing to receive."[17] Realizing our eternal destiny is dependent on our choices. It requires making and keeping sacred covenants. This covenant path is the way we come unto Christ and is based on absolute truth and eternal, unchanging law. We cannot create our own path and expect God's promised outcomes. To expect His blessings while not following the eternal laws upon which they are predicated[18] is misguided, like thinking we can touch a hot stove and "decide" not to be burned.

You may know that I used to treat patients with heart failure. Their best outcomes were obtained by following established, evidence-based treatment plans. Despite knowing this, some patients tried to negotiate a different treatment plan. They said, "I don't want to take so many medications" or "I don't want to undergo so many follow-up tests." Of course, patients were free to make their own decisions, but if they deviated from optimal treatment plans, their results suffered. Patients with heart failure cannot choose an inferior course and then blame their cardiologist for inferior outcomes.

The same is true for us. Heavenly Father's prescribed path leads to the best eternal outcomes. We are free to choose, but we cannot choose the consequences of not following the revealed path.[19] The Lord has said, "That which breaketh a law, and abideth not by law, but seeketh to become a law unto itself, . . . cannot be sanctified by law, neither by mercy, justice, nor judgment."[20] We cannot deviate from Heavenly Father's course and then blame Him for inferior outcomes.

The second paragraph in the Young Women theme reads: "As a

disciple of Jesus Christ, I strive to become like Him. I seek and act upon personal revelation and minister to others in His holy name." We can develop a testimony of Jesus Christ by acting in faith.[21] We can claim the spiritual gift "to know that Jesus Christ is the Son of God, and that he was crucified for the sins of the world." Or we can receive the gift to believe on the words of those who do know,[22] until we know for ourselves. We can follow the Savior's teachings and help others come unto Him. In this way, we join Him in His work.[23]

The Young Women theme continues, "I will stand as a witness of God at all times and in all things and in all places." All members of the Church are needed as witnesses of God,[24] although Apostles and Seventies are commissioned as special witnesses of the name of Christ.[25] Imagine a soccer match in which only the goalie protects the goal. Without the help of the other team players, the goalie will not be able to adequately defend the goal, and the team will always lose. So too, everyone is needed on the Lord's team.[26]

The final paragraph of the Young Women theme begins, "As I strive to qualify for exaltation, I cherish the gift of repentance and seek to improve each day." Because of the Savior's atoning sacrifice, we can repent, learn from our mistakes, and not be condemned by them. President Russell M. Nelson taught: "Too many people consider repentance as punishment. . . . But this feeling of being penalized is engendered by Satan. He tries to block us from looking to Jesus Christ, who stands with open arms, hoping and willing to heal, forgive, cleanse, strengthen, purify, and sanctify us."[27]

When we sincerely repent, no spiritual scar remains, no matter what we have done, how serious it was, or how many times we repeated it.[28] As often as we repent and seek forgiveness with real intent, we can be forgiven.[29] What a remarkable gift from our Savior, Jesus Christ![30] The Holy Ghost can assure us that we have been forgiven. As we sense joy and peace,[31] guilt is swept away,[32] and we are no longer tormented by our sin.[33]

Even after sincere repentance, however, we may stumble. Stumbling does not mean that the repentance was inadequate but may simply reflect human weakness. How comforting to know that "the Lord sees weaknesses differently than He [sees] rebellion." We should not doubt the Savior's ability to help us with our weaknesses, because "when the Lord speaks of weaknesses, it is always with mercy."[34]

The Young Women theme concludes, "With faith, I will strengthen my home and family, make and keep sacred covenants, and receive the ordinances and blessings of the holy temple." Strengthening home and family may mean forging the first link in a chain of faithfulness, carrying on a legacy of faith, or restoring it.[35] Regardless, strength comes through faith in Jesus Christ and by making sacred covenants.

In the temple, we learn who we are and where we have been. The Roman philosopher Cicero said, "To be ignorant of what occurred before you were born is to remain always a child."[36] He was, of course, referring to secular history, but his astute observation can be expanded. We live as perpetual children if we are ignorant of the eternal perspective gained in temples. There we grow up in the Lord, "receive a fulness of the Holy Ghost,"[37] and become more fully committed as disciples of the Savior.[38] As we keep our covenants, we receive God's power in our lives.[39]

I invite you to center your life on Jesus Christ and remember the foundational truths in the Young Women theme. If you are willing, the Holy Ghost will guide you. Our Heavenly Father wants you to become His heir and receive all that He has.[40] He cannot offer you more. He cannot promise you more. He loves you more than you know and wants you to be happy in this life and in the life to come. In the name of Jesus Christ, amen.

Notes

1. See Bonnie H. Cordon, "Beloved Daughters," *Ensign* or *Liahona*, Nov. 2019, 67; "Young Women Theme," ChurchofJesusChrist.org.
2. See also "The Family: A Proclamation to the World," ChurchofJesusChrist.org.
3. See Romans 8:35, 38–39.
4. See Galatians 5:22.
5. Richard G. Scott, "To Acquire Spiritual Guidance," *Ensign* or *Liahona*, Nov. 2009, 8. The jalapeño is a medium-sized chile pepper pod of the species *Capsicum annuum*.
6. See Mosiah 2:36.
7. See Gospel Topics, "Heavenly Parents," topics.ChurchofJesusChrist.org.

8. Dallin H. Oaks, "Apostasy and Restoration," *Ensign*, May 1995, 87; see also Doctrine and Covenants 131:1–4; 132:19. Women and men cannot be exalted without each other.

9. See Gospel Topics, "Heavenly Parents." Another resource providing information on this subject is the Gospel Topics essay "Mother in Heaven" (topics.ChurchofJesusChrist.org).

10. Even sincere questions about partially revealed or unrevealed truths can lead us to look "beyond the mark" (Jacob 4:14). In particular, we need to rely "wholly upon the merits of him who is mighty to save" (2 Nephi 31:19), Jesus Christ. Suggesting the need for something more than what Jesus Christ offers effectively diminishes the scope and power of His infinite Atonement. In so doing we divert our attention from the ultimate "source [to which we should] look for a remission of [our] sins" (2 Nephi 25:26).

11. 3 Nephi 18:19.

12. See, for example, Russell M. Nelson, "Lessons from the Lord's Prayers," *Ensign* or *Liahona*, May 2009, 47.

13. Numbers 16:28.

14. Numbers 22:18.

15. See Doctrine and Covenants 28:2–7.

16. See Gospel Topics, "Heavenly Parents."

17. Doctrine and Covenants 88:32.

18. See Doctrine and Covenants 130:20–21.

19. See 2 Nephi 2:5, 16, 26–27.

20. Doctrine and Covenants 88:35.

21. See Russell M. Nelson, "Christ Is Risen; Faith in Him Will Move Mountains," *Liahona*, May 2021, 101–4.

22. See Doctrine and Covenants 46:13–14.

23. See *General Handbook: Serving in The Church of Jesus Christ of Latter-day Saints*, 4.1, ChurchofJesusChrist.org.

24. See Mosiah 18:9.

25. See Doctrine and Covenants 27:12; 107:23, 25; 124:138–39.

26. No one needs to do everything, but everyone who is willing can do something. Moreover, God can make the willing able, but He cannot or will not make the able willing.

27. Russell M. Nelson, "We Can Do Better and Be Better," *Ensign* or *Liahona*, May 2019, 67.

28. Joseph Smith taught: "There is never a time when the spirit is too old to approach God. All are within the reach of pardoning mercy. . . . This doctrine appears glorious, inasmuch as it exhibits the greatness of divine compassion and benevolence in the extent of the plan of human salvation. This glorious truth is well calculated to enlarge the understanding, and to sustain the soul under troubles, difficulties and distress" (*Teachings of Presidents of the Church: Joseph Smith* [2007], 471). See also Boyd K. Packer, "The Plan of Happiness," *Ensign* or *Liahona*, May 2015, 28.

29. See Mosiah 26:29–30; Moroni 6:8; Doctrine and Covenants 58:42–43.

30. See Moroni 7:27–28. Remarkably, our Judge is also our Advocate.

31. See Mosiah 4:3.

32. See Enos 1:6.

33. See Alma 36:19.

34. Richard G. Scott, "Personal Strength through the Atonement of Jesus Christ," *Ensign* or *Liahona*, Nov. 2013, 83. Consciously planning a sin with the callous plan to repent afterwards—in other words, preplanned repentance—is repugnant to the Lord. Those who do so "crucify to themselves the Son of God afresh" (see Hebrews 6:4–6). This warning should be considered: "For if we sin wilfully after that we have received the knowledge of the truth, there remaineth no more sacrifice for sins, but a certain fearful looking for of judgment and fiery indignation" (Hebrews 10:26–27).

35. See Isaiah 58:12–14.

36. Marcus Tullius Cicero, *Orator*, trans. H. M. Hubbell, chapter 34, section 120; in *Cicero* (1971), 5:395.

37. See Doctrine and Covenants 109:15.

38. See Doctrine and Covenants 109:22.

39. See Doctrine and Covenants 84:19–20.

40. See Doctrine and Covenants 84:36–38.

SUNDAY
MORNING
SESSION

—

APRIL 3, 2022

OUR RELATIONSHIP WITH GOD

ELDER D. TODD CHRISTOFFERSON

Of the Quorum of the Twelve Apostles

As Job in the Old Testament, in a time of suffering some might feel that God has abandoned them. Because we know that God has power to prevent or remove any affliction, we may be tempted to complain if He does not do it, perhaps questioning, "If God does not grant the help I pray for, how can I have faith in Him?" At one point in his intense trials, righteous Job said:

"Then know that God has wronged me and drawn his net around me.

"Though I cry, 'I've been wronged!' I get no response; though I call for help, there is no justice."[1]

In His response to Job, God demands, "Wilt thou condemn me, that thou mayest be righteous?"[2] Or in other words, "Will you even put me in the wrong? Will you condemn me that you may be justified?"[3] Jehovah forcefully reminds Job of His omnipotence and omniscience, and Job in deepest humility admits he possesses nothing even close to the knowledge, power, and righteousness of God and cannot stand in judgment of the Almighty:

"I know that thou canst do every thing," he said, "and that no thought can be withholden from thee.

". . . I uttered that I understood not; things too wonderful for me, which I knew not. . . .

"Wherefore I abhor myself, and repent in dust and ashes."[4]

In the end, Job was privileged to see the Lord, and "the Lord blessed the latter end of Job more than his beginning."[5]

It truly is folly for us with our mortal myopia to presume to judge God, to think, for example, "I'm not happy, so God must be doing something wrong." To us, His mortal children in a fallen world, who know so little of past, present, and future, He declares, "All things are present with me, for I know them all."[6] Jacob wisely cautions: "Seek not to counsel the Lord, but to take counsel from his hand. For behold, ye yourselves know that he counseleth in wisdom, and in justice, and in great mercy, over all his works."[7]

Some misunderstand the promises of God to mean that obedience to Him yields specific outcomes on a fixed schedule. They might think, "If I diligently serve a full-time mission, God will bless me with a happy marriage and children," or "If I refrain from doing schoolwork on the Sabbath, God will bless me with good grades," or "If I pay tithing, God will bless me with that job I've been wanting." If life doesn't fall out precisely this way or according to an expected timetable, they may feel betrayed by God. But things are not so mechanical in the divine economy. We ought not to think of God's plan as a cosmic vending machine where we (i) select a desired blessing, (ii) insert the required sum of good works, and (iii) the order is promptly delivered.[8]

God will indeed honor His covenants and promises to each of us. We need not worry about that.[9] The atoning power of Jesus Christ—who descended below all things and then ascended on high[10] and who possesses all power in heaven and in earth[11]—ensures that God can and will fulfill His promises. It is essential that we honor and obey His laws, but not every blessing predicated on obedience to law[12] is shaped, designed, and timed according to our expectations. We do our best but must leave to Him the management of blessings, both temporal and spiritual.

President Brigham Young explained that his faith was not built on certain outcomes or blessings but on his witness of and relationship with Jesus Christ. He said: "My faith is not placed upon the Lord's working upon the islands of the sea, upon his bringing the people here, . . . nor upon the favors he bestows upon this people or upon that people, neither upon whether we are blessed or not blessed, but *my faith is placed upon the Lord Jesus Christ, and my knowledge I have received from him.*"[13]

Our repentance and obedience, our sacrifices, and our good works do matter. We want to be among those described by Ether as "always abounding in good works."[14] But it is not so much because of some tally kept in celestial account books. These things matter because they engage us in God's work and are the means by which we collaborate with Him in our own transformation from natural man to saint.[15] What our Heavenly Father offers us is Himself and His Son, a close and enduring relationship with Them through the grace and mediation of Jesus Christ, our Redeemer.

We are God's children, set apart for immortality and eternal life. Our destiny is to be His heirs, "joint-heirs with Christ."[16] Our Father is willing to guide each of us along His covenant path with steps designed to our individual need and tailored to His plan for our ultimate happiness with Him. We can anticipate a growing trust and faith in the Father and the Son, an increasing sense of Their love, and the consistent comfort and guidance of the Holy Spirit.

Even so, this path cannot be easy for any of us. There is too much refining needed for it to be easy. Jesus said:

"I am the true vine, and my Father is the husbandman.

"Every branch in me that beareth not fruit [the Father] taketh away: and every branch that beareth fruit, he purgeth it, that it may bring forth more fruit."[17]

The process of God-directed purging and purifying will, of necessity, be wrenching and painful at times. Recalling Paul's expression, we are "joint-heirs with Christ; *if so be that we suffer with him, that we may be also glorified together.*"[18]

So, in the midst of this refiner's fire, rather than get angry with God, get close to God. Call upon the Father in the name of the Son. Walk with Them in the Spirit, day by day. Allow Them over time to manifest Their fidelity to you. Come truly to know Them and truly to know yourself.[19] Let God prevail.[20] The Savior reassures us:

"Listen to him who is the advocate with the Father, who is pleading your cause before him—

"Saying: Father, behold the sufferings and death of him who did no sin, in whom thou wast well pleased; behold the blood of thy Son which was shed, the blood of him whom thou gavest that thyself might be glorified;

"*Wherefore, Father, spare these my brethren [and my sisters] that believe on my name, that they may come unto me and have everlasting life.*[21]

Consider some examples of faithful men and women who trusted God, confident that His promised blessings would be upon them in life or in death. Their faith was based not on what God did or did not do in a particular circumstance or moment in time but on knowing Him as their benevolent Father and Jesus Christ as their faithful Redeemer.

When Abraham was about to be sacrificed by the Egyptian priest of Elkenah, he cried out to God to save him, and God did.[22] Abraham lived to become the father of the faithful through whose seed all the families of the earth would be blessed.[23] Earlier, on this very same altar, that same priest of Elkenah had offered up three virgins who "because of their virtue . . . would not bow down to worship gods of wood or of stone."[24] They died there as martyrs.

Joseph of old, sold into slavery as a youth by his own brothers, in his anguish turned to God. Gradually, he rose to prominence in his master's house in Egypt but then had all his progress ripped away because of the false accusations of Potiphar's wife. Joseph could have thought, "So prison is what I get for keeping the law of chastity," but instead he again turned to God and was prospered even in prison. Joseph suffered a further disappointment when the prisoner he befriended, despite his promise to Joseph, forgot all about him after being restored to a position of trust in Pharaoh's court. Eventually, as you know, the Lord intervened to put Joseph in the highest position of trust and power next to Pharaoh, enabling Joseph to save the house of Israel and many others. Surely Joseph could attest "that all things work together for good to them that love God."[25]

Abinadi was intent on fulfilling his divine commission. "I finish my message," he said, "and then it matters not [what happens to me], if it so be that I am saved."[26] He was not spared a martyr's death, but assuredly he was saved in the kingdom of God, and his one precious convert, Alma, changed the course of Nephite history leading up to the coming of Christ.

Alma and Amulek were delivered from prison in Ammonihah

in answer to their plea, and their persecutors were slain.[27] Earlier, however, these same persecutors had cast believing women and their children into a raging fire. Alma, witnessing the horrific scene in agony was constrained by the Spirit not to exercise the power of God to "save them from the flames,"[28] that they might be received up to God in glory.[29]

The Prophet Joseph Smith languished in jail at Liberty, Missouri, powerless to help the Saints as they were pillaged and driven from their homes in the bitter cold of winter. "O God, where art thou?" Joseph cried. "How long shall thy hand be stayed?"[30] In response, the Lord promised: "Thine adversity and thine afflictions shall be but a small moment; and then if thou endure it well, God shall exalt thee on high. . . . Thou art not yet as Job."[31]

In the end, Joseph could declare with Job, "Though [God] slay me, yet will I trust in him."[32]

Elder Brook P. Hales related the story of Sister Patricia Parkinson, who was born with normal eyesight but by age 11 had gone blind.

Elder Hales recounted: "I've known Pat for many years and recently told her that I admired the fact that she is always positive and happy. She responded, 'Well, you have not been at home with me, have you? I have my moments. I've had rather severe bouts of depression, and I've cried a lot.' However, she added, 'From the time I started losing my sight, it was strange, but I knew that Heavenly Father and the Savior were with my family and me. . . . To those who ask me if I am angry because I am blind, I respond, 'Who would I be angry with? Heavenly Father is in this with me; I am not alone. He is with me all the time.'"[33]

In the end, it is the blessing of a close and abiding relationship with the Father and the Son that we seek. It makes all the difference and is everlastingly worth the cost. We will testify with Paul "that the sufferings of this present [mortal] time are not worthy to be compared with the glory which shall be revealed in us."[34] I bear witness that no matter what our mortal experience may entail, we can trust God and find joy in Him.

"Trust in the Lord with all thine heart; and lean not unto thine own understanding.

"In all thy ways acknowledge him, and he shall direct thy paths."[35]

In the name of Jesus Christ, amen.

Notes

1. Job 19:6–7, New International Version.
2. Job 40:8.
3. Job 40:8, New Revised Standard Version.
4. Job 42:2–3, 6.
5. Job 42:12.
6. Moses 1:6; see also Doctrine and Covenants 38:2.
7. Jacob 4:10.
8. King Benjamin taught that all God requires of us is to keep His commandments, "for which if ye do, he doth immediately bless you" (see Mosiah 2:22, 24). This does not mean, however, that all blessings come quickly. God's blessings are immediate in the sense that His commandments carry their own reward. It also means that obedience to His commandments brings the blessing of living in His presence by having His Holy Spirit with us (see Alma 36:30).
9. See Doctrine and Covenants 82:10.
10. See Doctrine and Covenants 88:6.
11. See Matthew 28:18.
12. See Doctrine and Covenants 130:20–21.
13. Brigham Young, "Instructions," *Deseret News*, Nov. 21, 1855, 290; emphasis added.
14. Ether 12:4.
15. See Mosiah 3:19; see also Dallin H. Oaks, "The Challenge to Become," *Ensign*, Nov. 2000, 32; *Liahona*, Jan. 2001, 40.
16. Romans 8:17.
17. John 15:1–2.
18. Romans 8:17; emphasis added.
19. See 1 Corinthians 13:12.
20. See Russell M. Nelson, "Let God Prevail," *Ensign* or *Liahona*, Nov. 2020, 92–95.
21. Doctrine and Covenants 45:3–5; emphasis added.
22. See Abraham 1:7, 15, 20.
23. See Abraham 2:11.
24. Abraham 1:11.
25. Romans 8:28.
26. Mosiah 13:9.
27. See Alma 14:23–28.
28. Alma 14:10.
29. Alma 14:11: "The Spirit constraineth me that I must not stretch forth mine hand; for behold the Lord receiveth them up unto himself, in glory; and he doth suffer that they may do this thing, or that the people may do this thing unto them, according to the hardness of their hearts, that the judgments which he shall exercise upon them in his wrath may be just; and the blood of the innocent shall stand as a witness against them, yea, and cry mightily against them at the last day."
30. Doctrine and Covenants 121:1–2.
31. Doctrine and Covenants 121:7–8, 10.
32. Job 13:15.
33. Brook P. Hales, "Answers to Prayer," *Ensign* or *Liahona*, May 2019, 14.
34. Romans 8:18.
35. Proverbs 3:5–6.

CHRIST HEALS THAT WHICH IS BROKEN

AMY A. WRIGHT

Second Counselor in the Primary General Presidency

A few years ago, at a family gathering, my then-eight-year-old nephew William asked our oldest son, Briton, if he would like to play ball with him. Briton enthusiastically responded, "Yes! I would love to!" After they had been playing for quite some time, a ball got away from Briton, and he accidentally broke one of his grand-parents' antique pots.

Briton felt awful. As he began picking up the broken pieces, William walked over to his cousin and lovingly patted him on the back. He then comforted, "Don't worry, Briton. I broke something at Grandma and Grandpa's house once, and Grandma put her arm around me and said, 'It's OK, William. You are only five.'"

To which Briton responded, "But, William, I'm 23!"

We can learn much from the scriptures about how our Savior, Jesus Christ, will help us successfully navigate the things in our lives that are broken, no matter our age. He can heal broken relationships with God, broken relationships with others, and broken parts of ourselves.

Broken Relationships with God

While the Savior was teaching in the temple, a woman was brought to Him by the scribes and Pharisees. We do not know her full story, just that she was "taken in adultery."[1] Often the scriptures give only a small portion of someone's life, and based on that por-tion, we sometimes tend to exalt or condemn. No one's life can be understood by one magnificent moment or one regrettable public disappointment. The purpose of these scriptural accounts is to help us see that Jesus Christ was the answer then, and He is the answer now. He knows our complete story and exactly what we suffer, as well as our capabilities and vulnerabilities.

Christ's response to this precious daughter of God was "Neither do I condemn thee: go, and sin no more."[2] Another way to say "go, and sin no more" could be "go forth and change." The Savior was inviting her to repent: to change her behavior, her associations, the way she felt about herself, her heart.

Because of Christ, our decision to "go forth and change" can also allow us to "go forth and heal," for He is the source of healing all that is broken in our lives. As the great Mediator and Advocate with the Father, Christ sanctifies and restores broken relationships— most important, our relationship with God.

The Joseph Smith Translation makes it clear that the woman *did* follow the Savior's counsel and changed her life: "And the woman glorified God from that hour, and believed on his name."[3] It is unfortunate that we do not know her name or other details about her life after this moment because it would have required great determination, humility, and faith in Jesus Christ for her to repent and change. What we do know is she was a woman who "believed on his name" with the understanding that she was not beyond the reach of His infinite and eternal sacrifice.

Broken Relationships with Others

In Luke chapter 15 we read a parable of a man who had two sons. The younger son asked his father for his inheritance, took his journey into a far country, and wasted his substance with riotous living.[4]

"And when he had spent all, there arose a mighty famine in that land; and he began to be in want.

"And he went and joined himself to a citizen of that country; and he sent him into his fields to feed swine.

"And he would fain have filled his belly with the husks that the swine did eat: and no man gave unto him.

"And when he came to himself, he said, How many hired servants of my father's have bread enough and to spare, and I perish with hunger!

"I will arise and go to my father, and will say unto him, Father, I have sinned against heaven, and before thee,

"And am no more worthy to be called thy son: make me as one of thy hired servants.

"And he arose, and came to his father. But when he was yet a great way off, his father saw him, and had compassion, and ran, and fell on his neck, and kissed him."[5]

The fact that the father ran to his son, I believe, is significant. The personal hurt that the son had inflicted upon his father was surely deep and profound. Likewise, the father may have been genuinely embarrassed by his son's actions.

So why didn't the father wait for his son to apologize? Why didn't he hold out for an offering of restitution and reconciliation before extending forgiveness and love? This is something I have often pondered.

The Lord teaches us that forgiving others is a universal commandment: "I, the Lord, will forgive whom I will forgive, but of you it is required to forgive all men."[6] Extending forgiveness can take tremendous courage and humility. It can also take time. It requires us to put our faith and trust in the Lord as we assume accountability for the condition of our hearts. Here lies the significance and power of our agency.

With the depiction of this father in the parable of the prodigal son, the Savior emphasized that forgiveness is one of the noblest gifts we can give one another and most specifically *ourselves*. Unburdening our hearts through forgiveness isn't always easy, but through the enabling power of Jesus Christ, it is possible.

Broken Parts of Ourselves

In Acts chapter 3 we learn about a man who was born lame and "whom they laid daily at the gate of the temple which is called Beautiful, to ask alms of them that entered into the temple."[7]

The lame beggar was over 40 years old[8] and had spent his entire life in a seemingly never-ending state of wanting and waiting, for he was dependent on the generosity of others.

One day he saw "Peter and John about to go into the temple [and] asked an alms.

"And Peter, fastening his eyes upon him with John, said, Look on us.

"And he gave heed unto them, expecting to receive something of them.

"Then Peter said, Silver and gold have I none; but such as I have give I thee: In the name of Jesus Christ of Nazareth rise up and walk.

"And he took him by the right hand, and lifted him up: and immediately his feet and ankle bones received strength.

"And he leaping up stood, and walked, and entered with them into the temple, walking, and leaping, and praising God."[9]

Oftentimes we can find ourselves, like the lame beggar at the gate of the temple, patiently—or sometimes impatiently—"wait[ing] upon the Lord."[10] Waiting to be healed physically or emotionally. Waiting for answers that penetrate the deepest part of our hearts. Waiting for a miracle.

Waiting upon the Lord can be a sacred place—a place of polishing and refining where we can come to know the Savior in a deeply personal way. Waiting upon the Lord may also be a place where we find ourselves asking, "O God, where art thou?"[11]—a place where spiritual perseverance requires us to exercise faith in Christ by intentionally choosing Him again and again and again. I know this place, and I understand this type of waiting.

I spent countless hours at a cancer treatment facility, united in my suffering with many who were yearning to be healed. Some lived; others did not. I learned in a profound way that deliverance from our trials is different for each of us, and therefore our focus should be less about the *way* in which we are delivered and more about the Deliverer Himself. Our *emphasis* should always be on Jesus Christ!

Exercising faith in Christ means trusting not only in God's will but also in His timing. For He knows exactly what we need and precisely when we need it. When we submit to the will of the Lord, we will ultimately receive substantially more than that which we had desired.

My dear friends, we all have something in our lives that is

broken that needs to be mended, fixed, or healed. As we turn to the Savior, as we align our hearts and minds with Him, as we repent, He comes to us "with healing in his wings,"[12] puts His arms lovingly around us, and says, "It's OK. You are only 5—or 16, 23, 48, 64, 91. We can fix this together!"

I testify that there is nothing in your life that is broken that is beyond the curative, redeeming, and enabling power of Jesus Christ. In the sacred and holy name of He who is mighty to heal, Jesus Christ, amen.

Notes

1. John 8:4.
2. John 8:11.
3. Joseph Smith Translation, John 8:11 (in John 8:11, footnote *c*).
4. See Luke 15:11–13.
5. Luke 15:14–20.
6. Doctrine and Covenants 64:10.
7. Acts 3:2.
8. See Acts 4:22.
9. Acts 3:3–8.
10. Isaiah 40:31.
11. Doctrine and Covenants 121:1.
12. 2 Nephi 25:13.

LOVE, SHARE, INVITE

ELDER GARY E. STEVENSON

Of the Quorum of the Twelve Apostles

Imagine with me, for a moment, standing on a mountain in Galilee, witnessing the wonder and glory of the resurrected Savior visiting His disciples. How awe-inspiring to consider personally hearing these words, which He shared with them, His solemn charge to "go ye therefore, and teach all nations, baptizing them in the name of the Father, and of the Son, and of the Holy Ghost."[1] Surely these words would empower, inspire, and move each of us, as they did His Apostles. Indeed, they devoted the rest of their lives to doing just that.

Interestingly, it wasn't only the Apostles who took Jesus's words to heart. Members of the early Church, from the newest to the most seasoned, took part in the Savior's great commission, sharing the good news of the gospel with those they met and knew. The determination to share their testimony of Jesus Christ helped His newly established Church grow expansively.[2]

We too, as Christ's disciples, are invited to heed His commission today, as if we were there on that mountain in Galilee when He first proclaimed it. This commission began again in 1830, when Joseph Smith set apart his brother Samuel as an early missionary of the Church of Jesus Christ.[3] Since that time, more than 1.5 million missionaries have traveled throughout the world teaching all nations and baptizing those who embrace the glad tidings of the restored gospel.

This is our doctrine. Our fond desire.

From our young children to the eldest among us, we yearn for the time when we can heed the Savior's call and share the gospel with the nations of the world. I am sure you young men and young women felt a similar empowering challenge from our prophet yesterday as he invited you to prepare for full-time missionary service just as the Savior did with His Apostles.

Like sprinters at the starting blocks, we wait with anticipation for the official invitation, complete with the prophet's signature, signaling the start of the race! This desire is noble and inspirational; however, let's consider this question: why don't we *all* begin now?

You might ask, "How can I be a missionary without a name badge?" Or we tell ourselves, "The full-time missionaries are set apart to do this work. I would like to help but perhaps later when life has calmed down a bit."

Brothers and sisters, it is much simpler than that! Gratefully, the Savior's great commission can be accomplished through simple, easily understandable principles taught to each of us from childhood: love, share, and invite.

Love

The first thing we can do is love as Christ loved.

Our hearts are heavy with the human suffering and tensions that we see throughout the world during these tumultuous times. However, we can be also inspired by the outpouring of compassion and humanitarianism that has been demonstrated by people everywhere through their efforts to reach out to the marginalized—those displaced from their homes, separated from their families, or experiencing other forms of sorrow and despair.

Recently, news sources reported how a group of mothers in Poland, out of concern for desperate, fleeing families, left fully equipped strollers on a train station platform in a neat line, ready and waiting for refugee mothers and children who would need them at that border crossing as they deboarded a train. Surely, our Heavenly Father smiles upon acts of selfless charity such as these, for as we bear one another's burdens, we "fulfil the law of Christ."[4]

Whenever we show Christlike love toward our neighbor, we preach the gospel—even if we do not voice a single word.

Love for others is the eloquent expression of the second great commandment to love our neighbor;[5] it shows the refining process of the Holy Spirit working within our own souls. By demonstrating Christ's love to others, we may cause those who see our good works to "glorify [our] Father which is in heaven."[6]

We do this expecting nothing in return.

Our hope, of course, is they will accept our love and our message, though how they react is not within our control.

What we do and who we are certainly are.

Through Christlike love for others, we preach the glorious, life-transforming properties of Christ's gospel, and we participate significantly in the fulfilling of His great commission.

Share

The second thing we can do is share.

During the early months of the COVID-19 pandemic, Brother Wisan from Thailand felt prompted to share his feelings and impressions of what he was learning in his study of the Book of Mormon on his social media account. In one of his particularly personal posts, he shared a story of two Book of Mormon missionaries, Alma and Amulek.

His brother, Winai, although set in his religious beliefs, was touched by the post and responded, unexpectedly asking, "Can I get that book in Thai?"

Wisan wisely arranged for a copy of the Book of Mormon to be delivered by two sister missionaries, who began teaching his brother.

Wisan joined in virtual lessons, during which he shared his feelings about the Book of Mormon. Winai learned to pray and study with a truth-seeking spirit, to accept and embrace the truth. Within months, Winai was baptized!

Wisan later said, "We have a responsibility to be an instrument in the hands of God, and we must be always ready for Him to do His work in His way through us." Their family miracle came because Wisan simply shared the gospel in a normal and natural way.

We all share things with others. We do it often. We share what movies and food we like, funny things we see, places we visit, art we appreciate, quotes we're inspired by.

How might we simply add to the list of things we already share what we love about the gospel of Jesus Christ?

Elder Dieter F. Uchtdorf explained: "If someone asks about

your weekend, don't hesitate to talk about what you experienced at church. Tell about the little children who stood in front of a congregation and sang with eagerness how they are trying to be like Jesus. Talk about the group of youth who spent time helping the elderly in rest homes to compile personal histories."[7]

Sharing isn't about "selling" the gospel. You don't have to write a sermon or correct someone's incorrect perceptions.

When it comes to missionary work, God doesn't need you to be His sheriff; He does, however, ask that you be His sharer.

By sharing our positive experiences in the gospel with others, we take part in fulfilling the Savior's great commission.

Invite

The third thing you can do is invite.

Sister Mayra is a recent convert from Ecuador. Her joy in the gospel skyrocketed immediately following her baptism as she invited friends and loved ones around her through social media accounts. Many family members and friends who saw her posts responded with questions. Mayra connected with them, often inviting them to her home to meet with the missionaries together.

Mayra's parents, her siblings, her aunt, two cousins, and several of her friends were baptized because she courageously invited them to "come and see," "come and serve," and "come and belong." Through her normal and natural invitations, over 20 people have accepted her invitation to be baptized members of the Church of Jesus Christ. This came about because Sister Mayra simply invited others to experience the joy she felt as a member of the Church.

There are hundreds of invitations we can extend to others. We can invite others to "come and see" a sacrament service, a ward activity, an online video that explains the gospel of Jesus Christ. "Come and see" can be an invitation to read the Book of Mormon or visit a new temple during its open house prior to its dedication. Sometimes the invitation is something we extend inward—an invitation to ourselves, giving us awareness and vision of opportunities surrounding us to act upon.

In our digital age, members often share messages through social media. There are hundreds, if not thousands, of uplifting things you might find worthy of sharing. This content offers invitations to "come and see," "come and serve," and "come and belong."

As we invite others to learn more about the gospel of Jesus Christ, we take part in the Savior's call to engage in the work of His commission.

Conclusion

My beloved brothers and sisters, we have spoken today of three simple things—easy things—that anyone can do. Things *you* can do! Perhaps you are already doing them—even without fully realizing that you are!

I invite you to consider ways you can love, share, and invite. As you do so, you will feel a measure of joy knowing that you are heeding the words of our beloved Savior.

What I am urging you to do is not a new program. You have heard these principles before. This is not the "next big thing" the Church is asking you to do. These three things are merely an extension of who we already are as disciples of Jesus Christ.

No name badge or letter is required.

No formal calling is needed.

As these three things become a natural part of who we are and how we live, they will become an automatic, unforced expression of genuine love.

Like those disciples of Christ who gathered together to learn from Him in Galilee 2,000 years ago, we too can embrace the Savior's charge and go into all the world preaching the gospel.

As we love, share, and invite, we take part in that great and glorious work that prepares the earth for the return of its Messiah.

That we may heed the Savior's call and strive to engage in His great commission is my prayer in the name of Jesus the Christ, amen.

Notes

1. Matthew 28:19.
2. What was the cause of the growth of the early Church? One historian suggests: "The first thing that would have elicited serious inquiry concerning the nature of the faith was personal contact with other believers. . . . To live and work alongside those who followed Jesus, to witness their behavior at close quarters, and to listen as they talked about the gospel amid their ordinary daily activities was to be confronted by the evidence of changed lives. In this sense, the drawing power of the Christian faith must often have consisted not so much in the public declarations of its most prominent representatives as in the quiet testimony of ordinary worshipers of Jesus witnessing to the credibility of their commitment by their integrity, constancy, and openness to others" (Ivor J. Davidson, *The Birth of the Church: From Jesus to Constantine, AD 30–312* [2005], 108–9).
3. See Lucy Mack Smith, History, 1845, page 169, josephsmithpapers.org.
4. Galatians 6:2.
5. See Matthew 22:39.
6. Matthew 5:16.
7. Dieter F. Uchtdorf, "Missionary Work: Sharing What Is in Your Heart," *Ensign* or *Liahona*, May 2019, 17.

FOR GOD SO LOVED US

ELDER MICHAEL T. RINGWOOD
Of the Seventy

"For God so loved the world, that he gave his only begotten Son, that whosoever believeth in him should not perish, but have everlasting life" (John 3:16). The first time I noticed this verse, I was not at church or in family home evening. I was watching a sporting event on television. No matter what station I watched, and no matter what game it was, at least one person held a sign that read "John 3:16."

I have come to equally love verse 17: "For God sent not his Son into the world to condemn the world; but that the world through him might be saved."

God sent Jesus Christ, His only Son in the flesh, to lay down His life for every one of us. This He did because He loves us and designed a plan for each of us to return home to Him.

But this is not a blanket, catchall, hit-or-miss sort of plan. It is personal, set forth by a loving Heavenly Father, who knows our hearts, our names, and what He needs us to do. Why do we believe that? Because we are taught it in the holy scriptures.

Moses repeatedly heard Heavenly Father speak the words "Moses, my son" (see Moses 1:6; see also verses 7, 40). Abraham learned he was a child of God, chosen for his mission even before he was born (see Abraham 3:12, 23). By the hand of God, Esther was placed in a position of influence to save her people (see Esther 4). And God trusted a young woman, a servant, to testify of a living prophet so Naaman could be healed (see 2 Kings 5:1–15).

I especially love that good man, short in stature, who climbed a tree to see Jesus. The Savior knew he was there, stopped, looked up into the branches, and spoke these words: "Zacchaeus, . . . come down" (Luke 19:5). And we cannot forget the 14-year-old who went into a grove of trees and learned how personal the plan really is: "[Joseph,] *this is My Beloved Son. Hear Him!*" (Joseph Smith—History 1:17).

Brothers and sisters, we are the focus of Heavenly Father's plan and the reason for our Savior's mission. Each of us, individually, is Their work and Their glory.

To me, no book of scripture illustrates this more clearly than has my study of the Old Testament. Chapter after chapter we discover examples of how Heavenly Father and Jehovah are intimately involved in our lives.

We have recently been studying about Joseph, the beloved son of Jacob. From his youth, Joseph was highly favored of the Lord, yet he experienced great trials at the hands of his brothers. Two weeks ago, many of us were touched by how Joseph forgave his brothers. In *Come, Follow Me* we read: "In many ways, Joseph's life parallels that of Jesus Christ. Even though our sins caused Him great suffering, the Savior offers forgiveness, delivering all of us from a fate far worse than famine. Whether we need to receive forgiveness or extend it—at some point we all need to do both—Joseph's example points us to the Savior, the true source of healing and reconciliation."[1]

A lesson I love in that account comes from Joseph's brother Judah, who played a part in God's personal plan for Joseph. When Joseph was betrayed by his brothers, Judah convinced them not to take Joseph's life but to sell him into slavery (see Genesis 37:26–27).

Many years later, Judah and his brothers needed to take their youngest brother, Benjamin, to Egypt. Initially their father resisted. But Judah made a promise to Jacob—he would bring Benjamin home.

In Egypt, Judah's promise was put to the test. Young Benjamin was wrongly accused of a crime. Judah, true to his promise, offered to be jailed in Benjamin's place. "For," he said, "how shall I go up to my father, and the lad be not with me?" (see Genesis 44:33–34). Judah was determined to keep his promise and return Benjamin safely. Do you ever feel about others the way Judah felt toward Benjamin?

Isn't this how parents feel about their children? How missionaries feel about people they serve? How Primary and youth leaders feel about those they teach and love?

No matter who you are or your current circumstances, someone feels exactly this way about you. Someone wants to return to Heavenly Father with you.

I am grateful for those who never give up on us, who continue to pour out their souls in prayer for us, and who continue to teach and help us qualify to return home to our Father in Heaven.

Recently a dear friend spent 233 days in the hospital with COVID-19. During that time, he was visited by his deceased father, who asked that a message be delivered to his grandchildren. Even from beyond the veil, this good grandfather desired to help his grandchildren return to their heavenly home.

Increasingly, disciples of Christ are remembering the "Benjamins" in their lives. Across the world they have heard the clarion call of God's living prophet, President Russell M. Nelson. Young men and young women are engaged in the Lord's youth battalion. Individuals and families are reaching out in a spirit of ministering—loving, sharing, and inviting friends and neighbors to come unto Christ. Youth and adults are remembering and striving to keep their covenants—filling God's temples, finding names of deceased family members, and receiving ordinances on their behalf.

Why does Heavenly Father's personalized plan for us include helping others return to Him? Because this is how we become like Jesus Christ. Ultimately, the account of Judah and Benjamin teaches us about the Savior's sacrifice for us. Through His Atonement, He gave His life to bring us home. Judah's words express the Savior's love: "How shall I go up to my father, and [you] be not with me?" As gatherers of Israel, those can be our words as well.

The Old Testament is packed with miracles and tender mercies that are the hallmark of Heavenly Father's plan. In 2 Kings 4, the phrase "it fell on a day" is used three times to emphasize to me that important events happen according to God's timing and no detail is too small for Him.

My new friend Paul testifies of this truth. Paul grew up in a home that was sometimes abusive and always intolerant of religion. While attending school on a military base in Germany, he noticed two sisters who seemed to have a spiritual light. Asking why they were different brought the answer that they belonged to The Church of Jesus Christ of Latter-day Saints.

Soon Paul began meeting with missionaries and was invited to church. The next Sunday, as he got off the bus, he noticed two men dressed in white shirts and ties. He asked them if they were elders of the Church. They answered yes, so Paul followed them.

During the service, a preacher pointed to people in the congregation and invited them to testify. At the end of each testimony, a drummer gave a drum salute and the congregation called out, "Amen."

When the preacher pointed to Paul, he stood up and said, "I know Joseph Smith was a prophet and the Book of Mormon is true." There was no drum salute or amens. Paul eventually realized he had gone to the wrong church. Soon, Paul found his way to the right place and was baptized.

On the day of Paul's baptism, a member he didn't know told him, "You saved my life." A few weeks earlier, this man had decided to look for another church and attended a service with drums and amens. When the man heard Paul bear his testimony of Joseph Smith and the Book of Mormon, he realized that God knew him, recognized his struggles, and had a plan for him. For both Paul and the man, "it fell on a day," indeed!

We too know that Heavenly Father has a personal plan of happiness for each of us. Because God sent His Beloved Son for us, the miracles we need will "[fall] on [the very] day" necessary for His plan to be fulfilled.

I testify that this year we can learn more about God's plan for us in the Old Testament. That sacred volume teaches the role of prophets in uncertain times and of God's hand in a world that was confused and often contentious. It is also about humble believers who faithfully looked forward to the coming of our Savior, just as we look forward to and prepare for His *Second* Coming—His long-prophesied, glorious return.

Until that day, we may not see with our natural eyes the design of God for all aspects of our lives (see Doctrine and Covenants 58:3). But we can remember Nephi's response when faced with something he didn't understand: while he didn't know the meaning of all things, he knew that God loves His children (see 1 Nephi 11:17).

This is my witness on this beautiful Sabbath morning. May we write it on our hearts and allow it to fill our souls with peace, hope, and eternal joy: God so loved us that He sent His Only Begotten Son—not to condemn us, but to save us. In the name of Jesus Christ, amen.

Notes

1. *Come, Follow Me—For Individuals and Families: Old Testament 2022*, 51.

TO HEAL THE WORLD

ELDER RONALD A. RASBAND
Of the Quorum of the Twelve Apostles

Brothers and sisters, at this glorious Easter season we are so blessed to meet and receive counsel and direction from God's servants.

Sacred guidance and teachings from our Heavenly Father help us navigate life in these perilous times. As was prophesied, "fires, and tempests," "wars, rumors of wars, and earthquakes in divers places," "and all manner of abominations,"[1] "plague,"[2] "famines, and pestilences"[3] are ravaging families, communities, and even nations.

There is another scourge sweeping the globe: attacks on your and my religious freedom. This growing sentiment seeks to remove religion and faith in God from the public square, schools, community standards, and civic discourse. Opponents of religious freedom seek to impose restrictions on expressions of heartfelt convictions. They even criticize and ridicule faith traditions.

Such an attitude marginalizes people, devaluing personal principles, fairness, respect, spirituality, and peace of conscience.

What is religious freedom?

It is freedom of worship in all its configurations: freedom of assembly, freedom of speech, freedom to act on personal beliefs, and freedom for others to do the same. Religious freedom allows each of us to decide for ourselves what we believe, how we live and act according to our faith, and what God expects of us.

Efforts to curtail such religious liberty are not new. Throughout history, people of faith have suffered mightily at the hands of others. Members of The Church of Jesus Christ of Latter-day Saints are no different.

From our beginnings, many seeking God were drawn to this Church because of its teachings of divine doctrine, including faith in Jesus Christ and His Atonement, repentance, the plan of happiness, and the Second Coming of our Lord.

Opposition, persecution, and violence plagued our first latter-day prophet, Joseph Smith, and his followers.

Amidst the turmoil in 1842, Joseph published 13 fundamental tenets of the growing Church, including this one: "We claim the privilege of worshiping Almighty God according to the dictates of our own conscience, and allow all men the same privilege, let them worship how, where, or what they may."[4]

His statement is inclusive, liberating, and respectful. That is the essence of religious freedom.

The Prophet Joseph Smith also stated:

"I am bold to declare before Heaven that I am just as ready to die in defending the rights of a Presbyterian, a Baptist, or a good man of any other denomination; for the same principle which would trample upon the rights of the . . . Saints would trample upon the rights of the Roman Catholics, or of any other denomination who may be unpopular and too weak to defend themselves.

"It is a love of liberty [that] inspires my soul—civil and religious liberty to the whole of the human race."[5]

Still, early Church members were attacked and driven thousands of miles, from New York to Ohio to Missouri, where the governor issued an order that members of the Church "must be treated as enemies and must be exterminated or driven from the state."[6] They fled to Illinois, but the torment continued. A mob murdered the Prophet Joseph, thinking that killing him would destroy the Church and scatter the believers. But the faithful held firm. Joseph's successor, Brigham Young, led thousands in a forced exodus 1,300 miles (2,100 km) west to what is now the state of Utah.[7] My own ancestors were amongst those early pioneer settlers.

From those days of intense persecution, the Lord's Church has grown steadily to nearly 17 million members, with well over half living outside the United States.[8]

In April 2020 our Church celebrated the 200th anniversary of the Restoration of the gospel with a proclamation to the world, prepared by our First Presidency and Quorum of the Twelve Apostles.

It begins, "We solemnly proclaim that God loves His children in every nation of the world."[9]

Our beloved prophet, Russell M. Nelson, has further expressed:

"We believe in freedom, kindness, and fairness for all of God's children.

"We are all brothers and sisters, each one a child of a loving Father in Heaven. His Son, the Lord Jesus Christ, invites all to come to Him, 'black and white, bond and free, male and female' (2 Nephi 26:33)."[10]

Consider with me four ways that society and individuals benefit from religious freedom.

First. Religious freedom honors the first and second great commandments, placing God at the center of our lives. We read in Matthew:

"Thou shalt love the Lord thy God with all thy heart, and with all thy soul, and with all thy mind."[11]

"And the second is like unto it, Thou shalt love thy neighbour as thyself."[12]

Whether in a chapel, synagogue, mosque, or tin-roofed hut, Christ's disciples and all like-minded believers can express devotion to God by worship of Him and willingness to serve His children.

Jesus Christ is the perfect example of such love and service. During His ministry, He cared for the poor,[13] healed the sick[14] and the blind.[15] He fed the hungry,[16] opened His arms to little children,[17] and forgave those who wronged Him, even crucified Him.[18]

The scriptures describe that Jesus "went about doing good."[19] So must we.

Second. Religious freedom fosters expressions of belief, hope, and peace.

As a church, we join with other religions protecting people of all faiths and persuasions and their right to speak their convictions. This does not mean we accept their beliefs, nor they ours, but we have more in common than we have with those who desire to silence us.

I recently represented the Church at the annual G20 Interfaith Forum in Italy. I was encouraged, even buoyed up, when I met with government and faith leaders from around the world. I realized wounds and differences can be resolved and even healed when we honor God, the Father of us all, and Jesus Christ, His Son. The Great Healer of all is our Lord and Savior, Jesus Christ.

I had an interesting moment as I closed my talk. The previous seven speakers had not closed in any manner of a faith tradition or in the name of God. As I spoke, I thought, "Do I just say thank you and sit down, or do I close 'in the name of Jesus Christ'?" I remembered who I was, and I knew the Lord would have me say His name to conclude my message. So I did. Looking back, it was my opportunity to express my belief; and I had the freedom of religion to bear my witness of His holy name.

Third. Religion inspires people to help others.

When religion is given the space and freedom to flourish, believers perform simple and sometimes heroic acts of service. The ancient Jewish phrase "tikkun olam," meaning "to repair or heal the world," is being reflected today in the efforts of so many. We have partnered with Catholic Charities, known as Caritas Internationalis; Islamic Relief; and any number of Jewish, Hindu, Buddhist, Sikh, and Christian organizations like the Salvation Army and the National Christian Foundation. Together we serve millions in need, most recently by aiding refugees of war with tents, sleeping bags, and food supplies,[20] and providing vaccinations, including polio[21] and COVID.[22] The list of what is being done is long, but so are the needs.

No question, people of faith, working together, can make significant interventions. At the same time, one-on-one service is often unheralded but quietly changes lives.

I think of the example in Luke when Jesus Christ reached out to the widow of Nain. Jesus, accompanied by a group of followers, came upon the burial procession of the widow's only son. Without him, she was facing emotional, spiritual, and even financial ruin. Jesus, seeing her tearstained face, said, "Weep not."[23] Then He touched the bier carrying the body, and the procession halted.

"Young man," He commanded, "I say unto thee, Arise.

"And he that was dead sat up, and began to speak. And [Jesus] delivered him to his mother."[24]

Raising the dead is a miracle, but every act of kindness and concern for someone struggling is the covenant way each of us can also "[go] about doing good," knowing "God [is] with [us]."[25]

And **fourth.** Freedom of religion acts as a unifying and rallying force for shaping values and morality.

In the New Testament we read of many turning away from Jesus Christ, murmuring of His doctrine, "This is an hard saying; who can hear it?"[26]

That cry is still being heard today from those who seek to expel religion from discourse and influence. If religion is not there to help with shaping character and mediating hard times, who will be? Who will teach honesty, gratitude, forgiveness, and patience? Who will exhibit charity, compassion, and kindness for the forgotten and the downtrodden? Who will embrace those who are different yet deserving, as are all of God's children? Who will open their arms to those in need and seek no recompense? Who will reverence peace and obedience to laws greater than the trends of the day? Who will respond to the Savior's plea "Go, and do thou likewise"?[27]

We will! Yes, brothers and sisters, we will.

I invite you to champion the cause of religious freedom. It is an expression of the God-given principle of agency.

Religious freedom brings balance to competing philosophies. The good of religion, its reach, and the daily acts of love which religion inspires only multiply when we protect the freedom to express and act on core beliefs.

I witness that Russell M. Nelson is God's living prophet. I testify that Jesus Christ leads and guides this Church. He atoned for our sins, was crucified on a cross, and was resurrected on the third day.[28] Because of Him, we can live again for all eternity; and those who so desire can be with our Father in Heaven. This truth I proclaim to all the world. I am grateful for the freedom to do so. In the name of Jesus Christ, amen.

Notes

1. Mormon 8:29–31; see also 2 Timothy 3:1–7, 12–13; Doctrine and Covenants 45:26–27.
2. Doctrine and Covenants 87:6.
3. Matthew 24:7.
4. Articles of Faith 1:11.
5. *Teachings of Presidents of the Church: Joseph Smith* (2007), 345.
6. Lilburn W. Boggs letter to John B. Clark, Oct. 27, 1838, Mormon War Papers, Missouri State Archives, Jefferson City, Missouri, sos.mo.gov/archives/resources/Mormon.
7. See *Saints: The Story of the Church of Jesus Christ in the Latter Days*, vol. 2, *No Unhallowed Hand, 1846–1893* (2020), 3–68.
8. Member and Statistical Records Department figures for 2021 year-end: 16.8 million total members; US and Canada: 7 million members; outside the US and Canada: 9.8 million members.
9. "The Restoration of the Fulness of the Gospel of Jesus Christ: A Bicentennial Proclamation to the World," ChurchofJesusChrist.org; read by President Russell M. Nelson as part of his Sunday morning message at the 190th Annual General Conference, Apr. 5, 2020.
10. Russell M. Nelson, "Jesus Said Love Everyone," *Friend*, Apr. 2021, 2.
11. Matthew 22:37.
12. Matthew 22:39.
13. See Mark 10:21–22; 12:41–44; Luke 16:19–25.
14. See Luke 4:40; 8:43–48.
15. See John 9:1–7.
16. See Matthew 14:15–21; 15:32–38; Mark 6:31–44; 8:6–9; John 6:1–14.
17. See Matthew 19:13–15.
18. See Luke 23:33–34.
19. Acts 10:38.
20. See Mary Richards, "How the Church Is Helping with Humanitarian Aid in Eastern Europe," *Church News*, Mar. 3, 2022, thechurchnews.com.
21. See Sarah Ferguson, "Wild Polio Eliminated in Africa: A Giant Step Closer to Eradication," UNICEF, Oct. 22, 2020, unicefusa.org.
22. See Peggy Fletcher Stack, "LDS Church Kicks In $20M toward Global COVID Vaccination Push," *Salt Lake Tribune*, Feb. 26, 2021, sltrib.com.
23. Luke 7:13.
24. Luke 7:14–15.
25. Acts 10:38.
26. John 6:60.
27. Luke 10:37.
28. See 1 Corinthians 15:4.

TEACHING SELF-RELIANCE TO CHILDREN AND YOUTH

ELDER HUGO E. MARTINEZ
Of the Seventy

I will speak about self-reliance and how it can be taught to children and to youth. Self-reliance may be perceived as being subject matter for adults. I've come to know that adults can best be on the path toward self-reliance when they have been taught the gospel of Jesus Christ and have practiced its doctrine and principles since childhood and as youth in the home.

The best illustration is a great real-life example. Wilfried Vanie, his seven siblings, and his mother joined the Church in Abidjan, Ivory Coast, when he was six years old. He was baptized at eight. His father, the main provider in the family, died when Wilfried was eleven.

Though saddened by the family situation, Wilfried decided to continue in school, with his mother's encouragement and with Church support. He graduated from secondary school and served a full-time mission in the Ghana Cape Coast Mission, where he learned English. After his mission, he went on to the university and obtained a diploma in accounting and finance. Though it was hard to obtain employment in this field, he found work in the tourism and hospitality industry.

He started as a waiter in a five-star hotel, but his passion to improve pushed him to learn more until he became a bilingual receptionist there. When a new hotel opened, he was hired as the night auditor. Later, he enrolled in BYU–Pathway Worldwide and is currently studying a course to obtain a certificate in hospitality and tourism management. His desire is to one day become the manager of a high-end hotel. Wilfried can provide for his eternal companion and two children, as well as help his mother and his siblings. He currently serves in the Church as a member of the stake high council.

Self-reliance is defined as "the ability, commitment, and effort to provide the spiritual and temporal necessities of life for self and family."[1] Striving to be self-reliant is part of our work along the covenant path that leads us back to Heavenly Father and to His Son, Jesus Christ. It will strengthen our faith in Jesus Christ and joyfully bind us to Him through the covenants and ordinances of salvation and exaltation. Self-reliance is a doctrine of the gospel of Jesus Christ, not a program. It is a process that lasts a lifetime, not an event.

We become self-reliant throughout our lives by growing in spiritual strength, improving our physical and emotional health, pursuing our education and employment, and being temporally prepared.[2] Is this task ever finished during our lives? *No*, it is a lifelong process of learning, growth, and work. It never ends; it is a continuous, daily process.

How can we teach the doctrine and principles of self-reliance to our children and youth? One important way is to regularly apply the principles of the Children and Youth program. Parents and children learn the gospel of Jesus Christ, participate in service and activities, and work together in four areas of personal development that are unique for each child. It is no longer the same prescribed program for all.

The *Children's Guidebook* says: "When Jesus was your age, He learned and grew. You are learning and growing too. The scriptures say: 'Jesus increased in wisdom and stature, and in favour with God and man' (Luke 2:52)."[3] This scripture refers to growth and learning in the spiritual aspect, favor with God; the social aspect, favor with man; the physical aspect, stature; and the intellectual aspect, wisdom. These developmental areas apply to all of us, no matter our age. When do we teach them? In Deuteronomy 6:6–7 we read:

"And these words, which I command thee this day, shall be in thine heart:

"And thou shalt teach them diligently unto thy children, and shalt talk of them when thou sittest in thine house, and when thou walkest by the way, and when thou liest down, and when thou risest up."

We teach these things to children by our good example, by

working and serving with them, studying the scriptures, and following the teachings of Jesus Christ as taught by prophets.

I've mentioned that in the Children and Youth program, children choose different goals in each one of the four areas of development. It is important that they create their own goals in each area. Parents and leaders can teach, counsel, and support.

For example, our granddaughter Miranda is very motivated to grow spiritually by participating in daily early-morning seminary classes. She became interested by hearing positive comments from other seminary students in her ward. Her mother does not have to wake her up for class. On her own, she is up and connected by videoconference at the appointed time of 6:20 in the morning because she has developed good habits that help her to do so. My own parents told me recently that Miranda now talks more when she visits them, as she has grown in self-confidence. These are lessons for life and growth with noticeable outcomes.

Parents, grandparents, leaders, and friends assist in the growth and development of the children. Fully engaged ministering brothers and sisters, together with priesthood and organization leaders of the ward, provide support. "The Family: A Proclamation to the World" says: "By divine design, fathers are to preside over their families in love and righteousness and are responsible to provide the necessities of life and protection for their families. Mothers are primarily responsible for the nurture of their children. In these sacred responsibilities, fathers and mothers are obligated to help one another as equal partners. . . . Extended families should lend support when needed."[4] That last line refers to grandparents, among others.

As we serve in West Africa, my wife, Nuria, has done a remarkable job ministering to and remaining connected with our family and grandchildren across the ocean. She does this by using technology. She reads books to the younger grandchildren. She teaches the older granddaughters topics like the story of our family, science, the history of Puerto Rico, the Articles of Faith, and the gospel of Jesus Christ. Distances nowadays do not limit connecting, belonging, and ministering to and teaching the rising generation of our families.

I also join in with Nuria when I can to teach our precious grandchildren, to love them, and to spoil them and make them laugh.

You should notice the inspired similarities between the Children and Youth program and building self-reliance. The four areas of development in each are very similar. Spiritual strength in self-reliance relates to the spiritual in Children and Youth. Physical and emotional health in self-reliance connect with the physical and social in Children and Youth. Education, employment, and temporal preparedness in self-reliance are akin to the intellectual in the Children and Youth program.

In closing, let us follow our Savior, Jesus Christ, and His gospel by becoming self-reliant throughout our lives and teaching this to our children and youth. We can do this best by

1. being good examples of service to others,
2. living and teaching the doctrine and principles of self-reliance, and
3. obeying the commandment to build self-reliance as part of the gospel of Jesus Christ.

Doctrine and Covenants 104:15–16 says:

"It is my purpose to provide for my saints, for all things are mine.

"But it must needs be done in mine own way; and behold this is the way that I, the Lord, have decreed to provide for my saints, that the poor shall be exalted, in that the rich are made low."

This is the Church of Jesus Christ. His gospel blesses families here on earth and throughout the eternities. It guides us in our lives as we strive to become eternal families. I know this is true. In the name of Jesus Christ, amen.

Notes

1. *General Handbook: Serving in The Church of Jesus Christ of Latter-day Saints*, 22.0, ChurchofJesusChrist.org.
2. See *General Handbook*, 22.1.
3. *Personal Development: Children's Guidebook* (2019), 4.
4. "The Family: A Proclamation to the World," ChurchofJesusChrist.org.

THE POWER OF SPIRITUAL MOMENTUM

PRESIDENT RUSSELL M. NELSON

President of The Church of Jesus Christ of Latter-day Saints

My dear brothers and sisters, I love you. I cherish this opportunity to speak with you today. I pray daily that you will be protected from the fierce attacks of the adversary and have the strength to push forward through whatever challenges you face.

Some trials are deeply private burdens no one else can see. Others are played out on the world stage. The armed conflict in eastern Europe is one of these. I have been to Ukraine and Russia many times. I love those lands, the people, and their languages. I weep and pray for all who are affected by this conflict. As a church we're doing all we can to help those who are suffering and struggling to survive. We invite everyone to continue to fast and pray for all the people being hurt by this calamity. Any war is a horrifying violation of everything the Lord Jesus Christ stands for and teaches.

None of us can control nations or the actions of others or even members of our own families. But we can control ourselves. My call today, dear brothers and sisters, is to end conflicts that are raging in *your* heart, *your* home, and *your* life. Bury any and all inclinations to hurt others—whether those inclinations be a temper, a sharp tongue, or a resentment for someone who has hurt you. The Savior commanded us to turn the other cheek,[1] to love our enemies, and to pray for those who despitefully use us.[2]

It can be painfully difficult to let go of anger that feels so justified. It can seem impossible to forgive those whose destructive actions have hurt the innocent. And yet, the Savior admonished us to "forgive all men."[3]

We are followers of the Prince of Peace. Now more than ever, we need the peace only He can bring. How can we expect peace to exist in the world when we are not *individually* seeking peace and harmony? Brothers and sisters, I know what I'm suggesting is not easy. But followers of Jesus Christ should set the example for all the world to follow. I plead with you to do all you can to end *personal* conflicts that are currently raging in your hearts and in your lives.

May I underscore this call to action by discussing a concept I was reminded of recently while watching a basketball game.

In that game, the first half was a seesaw battle, back and forth. Then, during the last five seconds of the first half, a guard on one team made a beautiful three-point shot. With only one second left, his teammate stole the inbound pass and made another basket at the buzzer! So that team went into the locker room four points ahead with a palpable surge of momentum. They were able to carry that momentum into the second half and win the game.

Momentum is a powerful concept. We all have experienced it in one form or another—for example, in a vehicle that picks up speed or with a disagreement that suddenly turns into an argument.

So I ask, what can ignite *spiritual momentum*? We have seen examples of both positive and negative momentum. We know followers of Jesus Christ who became converted and grew in their faith. But we also know of once-committed believers who fell away. Momentum can swing either way.

We have never needed *positive* spiritual momentum more than we do now, to counteract the speed with which evil and the darker signs of the times are intensifying. Positive spiritual momentum will keep us moving forward amid the fear and uncertainty created by pandemics, tsunamis, volcanic eruptions, and armed hostilities. Spiritual momentum can help us withstand the relentless, wicked attacks of the adversary and thwart his efforts to erode our personal spiritual foundation.

Many actions can ignite positive spiritual momentum. Obedience, love, humility, service, and gratitude[4] are but a few.

Today I would like to suggest five specific actions we can take to help us maintain positive spiritual momentum.

First: **Get on the covenant path and stay there.**

Not long ago, I had a vivid dream in which I met a large group of people. They asked me many questions, the most frequent of which was about the covenant path and why it is so important.

In my dream, I explained that we enter the covenant path by being baptized and making our first covenant with God.[5] Each time we partake of the sacrament, we promise *again* to take the name of the Savior upon us, to remember Him, and to keep His commandments.[6] In return, God assures us that we may *always* have the Spirit of the Lord to be with us.

Later we make additional covenants in the temple, where we receive even greater promises. Ordinances and covenants give us access to godly power. The covenant path is the *only* path that leads to exaltation and eternal life.

In my dream, a woman then asked how someone who has broken his or her covenants can get back on that path. My answer to her question leads to my second suggestion:

Discover the *joy* of daily repentance.

How important is repentance? Alma taught that we should "preach nothing save it were repentance and faith on the Lord."[7] Repentance is required of every accountable person who desires eternal glory.[8] There are no exceptions. In a revelation to the Prophet Joseph Smith, the Lord chastised early Church leaders for not teaching the gospel to their children.[9] Repenting is the *key* to progress. Pure faith keeps us moving forward on the covenant path.

Please do not fear or delay repenting. Satan delights in your misery. Cut it short. Cast his influence out of your life! Start today to experience the joy of putting off the natural man.[10] The Savior loves us always but *especially* when we repent. He promised that though "the mountains shall depart, and the hills be removed . . . *my kindness* shall not depart from thee."[11]

If you feel you have strayed off the covenant path too far or too long and have no way to return, that simply is not true.[12] Please contact your bishop or branch president. He is the Lord's agent and will help you experience the joy and relief of repenting.

Now, a caution: Returning to the covenant path does *not* mean that life will be easy. This path is rigorous and at times will feel like a steep climb.[13] This ascent, however, is designed to test and teach us, refine our natures, and help us to become saints. It is the *only* path that leads to exaltation. One prophet[14] described the "blessed and happy state of those that keep the commandments of God. For behold, they are blessed in all things, both temporal and spiritual; and if they hold out faithful to the end they are received into heaven . . . [and] dwell with God in a state of never-ending happiness."[15]

Walking the covenant path, coupled with daily repentance, fuels positive spiritual momentum.

My third suggestion: **Learn about God and how He works.**

One of our greatest challenges today is distinguishing between the truths of God and the counterfeits of Satan. That is why the Lord warned us to "pray always, . . . that [we] may conquer Satan, and . . . *escape the hands of the servants of Satan* that do uphold his work."[16]

Moses provided an example of how to discern between God and Satan. When Satan came tempting Moses, he detected the deception because he had just had a face-to-face interaction with God. Moses quickly realized who Satan was and commanded him to depart.[17] When Satan persisted, Moses knew how to call upon God for more help. Moses received divine strength and rebuked the evil one *again*, saying, "Depart from me, Satan, for this one God only will I worship."[18]

We should follow that example. Cast Satan's influence out of your life! Please do not *follow* him down to his "gulf of misery and endless wo."[19]

With frightening speed, a testimony that is not nourished daily "by the good word of God"[20] can crumble. Thus, the antidote to Satan's scheme is clear: we need daily experiences worshipping the Lord and studying His gospel. I plead with you to let God prevail in your life. Give Him a fair share of your time. As you do, notice what happens to your positive spiritual momentum.

Suggestion number 4: **Seek and expect miracles.**

Moroni assured us that "God has not ceased to be a God of miracles."[21] *Every* book of scripture demonstrates how willing the Lord is to intervene in the lives of those who believe in Him.[22] He parted the Red Sea for Moses, helped Nephi retrieve the brass plates, and restored His Church through the Prophet Joseph Smith. Each of these miracles took time and may not have been exactly what those individuals originally requested from the Lord.

In the same way, the Lord will bless *you* with miracles *if* you believe in Him, "doubting nothing."[23] Do the spiritual work to seek miracles. Prayerfully ask God to help you exercise that kind of faith. I promise that you can experience for yourself that Jesus Christ "giveth power to the faint; and to them that have no might he increaseth strength."[24] Few things will accelerate your spiritual momentum more than realizing the Lord is helping you to move a mountain in your life.

Suggestion number 5: **End conflict in your personal life.**

I repeat my call to end the conflicts in *your* life. Exercise the humility, courage, and strength required both to forgive and to seek forgiveness. The Savior has promised that "if [we] forgive men their trespasses, [our] heavenly Father will also forgive [us]."[25]

Two weeks from today we celebrate Easter. Between now and then, I invite you to seek an end to a personal conflict that has weighed you down. Could there be a more fitting act of gratitude to Jesus Christ for His Atonement? If forgiveness presently seems impossible, plead for power through the atoning blood of Jesus Christ to help you. As you do so, I promise personal peace and a burst of spiritual momentum.

When the Savior atoned for all mankind, He opened a way that those who follow Him can have access to His healing, strengthening, and redeeming power. These spiritual privileges are available to all who seek to hear Him and follow Him.

My dear brothers and sisters, with all the pleadings of my heart, I urge you to get on the covenant path and stay there. Experience the joy of repenting daily. Learn about God and how He works. Seek and expect miracles. Strive to end conflict in your life.

As you act on these pursuits, I promise you the ability to move forward on the covenant path with increased momentum, despite whatever obstacles you face. And I promise you greater strength to resist temptation, more peace of mind, freedom from fear, and greater unity in your families.

God lives! Jesus is the Christ! He lives! He loves us and will help us. Of this I testify in the sacred name of our Redeemer, Jesus Christ, amen.

Notes

1. See 3 Nephi 12:39.
2. See 3 Nephi 12:44.
3. Doctrine and Covenants 64:10; see also verse 9.
4. As the Apostle Paul said, "In every thing give thanks" (1 Thessalonians 5:18). One of the surest antidotes for despair, discouragement, and spiritual lethargy is gratitude. What are some things for which we can give thanks to God? Thank Him for the beauty of the earth, for the Restoration of the gospel, and for the countless ways He and His Son make Their power available to us here on this earth. Thank Him for the scriptures, for angels who respond to our pleas to God for help, for revelation, and for eternal families. And most of all, thank God for the gift of His Son and the Atonement of Jesus Christ, which makes it possible for us to fulfill the missions for which we have been sent to earth.
5. To understand the covenant path, it is important to understand that a covenant involves a two-way commitment between God and one of His children. In a covenant, God sets the terms, and we agree to those terms. In exchange, God makes promises to us. Many covenants are accompanied by outward signs—or sacred ordinances—in which we participate with witnesses present. For example, baptism is a sign to the Lord that the person being baptized has made a covenant to keep the commandments of God.
6. See Moroni 4:3; 5:2; Doctrine and Covenants 20:77, 79.
7. Mosiah 18:20.
8. See Moses 6:50, 57.
9. See Doctrine and Covenants 93:40–48.
10. See Mosiah 3:19.
11. Isaiah 54:10, emphasis added; see also 3 Nephi 22:10. *Kindness* is translated from the Hebrew term *hesed*, a powerful word with deep meaning that encompasses kindness, mercy, covenant love, and more.
12. It is possible to make restitution for some sins but not others. If one person abuses or assaults another, or if one takes the life of another, full restitution cannot be made. The sinner in those cases can only do so much, and a large balance is left owing. Because of the Lord's willingness to forgive a balance due, we can come to Him regardless of how far we have strayed. When we sincerely repent, He will forgive us. Any balance owing between our sins and our ability to make full restitution can be paid only by applying the Atonement of Jesus Christ, who can make a gift of mercy. His willingness to forgive our balance due is a priceless gift.
13. See 2 Nephi 31:18–20.
14. The Nephite prophet King Benjamin.
15. Mosiah 2:41.
16. Doctrine and Covenants 10:5; emphasis added.
17. See Moses 1:16; see also verses 1–20.
18. Moses 1:20.
19. Helaman 5:12.
20. Moroni 6:4.
21. Mormon 9:15; see also verse 19.
22. John the Apostle declared that he recorded the Savior's miracles so "that [we] might believe that Jesus is the Christ" (John 20:31).
23. Mormon 9:21.
24. Isaiah 40:29.
25. Matthew 6:14.

SUNDAY AFTERNOON SESSION

———

APRIL 3, 2022

DIVINE LOVE IN THE FATHER'S PLAN

PRESIDENT DALLIN H. OAKS
First Counselor in the First Presidency

The gospel plan shows our Heavenly Father's love for all His children. To understand this, we must seek to understand His plan and His commandments. He loves His children so much that He gave His Only Begotten Son, Jesus Christ, to be our Savior and Redeemer, to suffer and die for us. In the restored Church of Jesus Christ of Latter-day Saints, we have a unique understanding of our Heavenly Father's plan. This gives us a different way of viewing the purpose of mortal life, the divine judgment that follows it, and the ultimate glorious destiny of all of God's children.

I love you, my brothers and sisters. I love all of God's children. When Jesus was asked, "Which is the great commandment in the law?" He taught that to love God and to love our neighbors are the first of God's great commandments.[1] Those commands are first because they invite us to grow spiritually by seeking to imitate God's love for us. I wish we all had a better understanding of the loving doctrine and policies that our Heavenly Father and His Son, Jesus Christ, have established in The Church of Jesus Christ of Latter-day Saints. What I say here seeks to clarify how God's love explains that doctrine and the Church's inspired policies.

I.

A common misunderstanding of the judgment that ultimately follows mortal life is that good people go to a place called *heaven* and bad people go to an everlasting place called *hell*. This erroneous assumption of only two ultimate destinations implies that those who cannot keep all the commandments required for heaven will necessarily be forever destined for hell.

A loving Heavenly Father has a better plan for His children. The revealed doctrine of the restored Church of Jesus Christ teaches that *all the children of God*—with exceptions too limited to consider here—will finally wind up in a kingdom of *glory*.[2] "In my Father's house are many mansions,"[3] Jesus taught. From modern revelation we know that those mansions are in three different kingdoms of glory. In the Final Judgment each of us will be judged according to our deeds and the desires of our hearts.[4] Before that, we will need to suffer for our unrepented sins. The scriptures are clear on that.[5] Then our righteous Judge will grant us residence in one of those kingdoms of glory. Thus, as we know from modern revelation, all "shall be judged . . . , and every man shall receive according to his own works, his own dominion, in the mansions which are prepared."[6]

The Lord has chosen to reveal comparatively little about two of these kingdoms of glory. In contrast, the Lord has revealed much about the highest kingdom of glory, which the Bible describes as the "glory of the sun."[7]

In the "celestial" glory[8] there are three degrees, or levels.[9] The highest of these is exaltation in the celestial kingdom, wherein we may become like our Father and His Son, Jesus Christ. To help us develop the godly attributes and the change in nature necessary to realize our divine potential, the Lord has revealed doctrine and established commandments based on eternal law. This is what we teach in The Church of Jesus Christ of Latter-day Saints because the purpose of the doctrine and policies of this restored Church is to prepare God's children for salvation in the celestial glory and, more particularly, for exaltation in its highest degree.

The covenants made and the blessings promised to the faithful in the temples of God are the key. This explains our worldwide building of temples, about which the choir has sung so beautifully. Some are puzzled at this emphasis, not understanding that the covenants and ordinances of the temple guide us toward achieving exaltation. This can be understood only in the context of the revealed truth of *three* degrees of glory. Because of our Heavenly Father's great love for all of His children, He has provided other kingdoms of glory—as Elder Quentin L. Cook explained yesterday—all of which are more wonderful than we can comprehend.[10]

The Atonement of Jesus Christ makes all of this possible. He has revealed that He "glorifies the Father, and *saves all the works of his hands.*"[11] That salvation is granted in different kingdoms of glory. We know from modern revelation that "all kingdoms have a law given."[12] Significantly:

"He who is not able to abide the law of a celestial kingdom cannot abide a celestial glory.

"And he who cannot abide the law of a terrestrial kingdom cannot abide a terrestrial glory.

"And he who cannot abide the law of a telestial kingdom cannot abide a telestial glory."[13]

In other words, the kingdom of glory we receive in the Final Judgment is determined by the laws we choose to abide by in our Heavenly Father's loving plan. Under that plan there are multiple kingdoms so that all of His children can be assigned to a kingdom where they can "abide."

II.

The teachings and policies of the Lord's restored Church apply these eternal truths in a way that can be fully understood only in the context of our Heavenly Father's loving plan for *all* of His children.

Thus, we honor individual agency. Most are aware of this Church's great efforts to promote religious freedom. These efforts are in furtherance of our Heavenly Father's plan. We seek to help *all* of His children—not just our own members—enjoy the precious freedom to choose.

Similarly, we are sometimes asked why we send missionaries to so many nations, even among Christian populations. We are also asked why we give enormous humanitarian aid to persons who are not members of our Church without linking this to our missionary efforts. We do this because the Lord has taught us to esteem all of His children as our brothers and sisters, and we want to share our spiritual and temporal abundance with everyone.

Eternal doctrine also provides a distinctive perspective on children. Through this perspective we see the bearing and nurturing of children as part of the divine plan. It is a joyful and sacred duty of those given the power to participate in it. Therefore, we are commanded to teach and contend for principles and practices that provide the best conditions for the development and happiness of children under God's plan.

III.

Finally, The Church of Jesus Christ of Latter-day Saints is properly known as a family-centered Church. But not well understood is the reality that our family-centeredness is not limited to mortal relationships. Eternal relationships are also fundamental to our theology. The mission of the restored Church is to help all the children of God qualify for what God desires as their ultimate destiny. By the redemption provided through the Atonement of Christ, all may attain eternal life (exaltation in the celestial kingdom), which Mother Eve declared "God giveth unto all the obedient."[14] This is more than salvation. President Russell M. Nelson has reminded us that "in God's eternal plan, salvation is an individual matter; [but] exaltation is a family matter."[15]

Fundamental to us is God's revelation that exaltation can be attained only through faithfulness to the covenants of an eternal marriage between a man and a woman.[16] That divine doctrine is why we teach that "gender is an essential characteristic of individual premortal, mortal, and eternal identity and purpose."[17]

That is also why the Lord has required His restored Church to oppose social and legal pressures to retreat from His doctrine of marriage between a man and a woman, to oppose changes that homogenize the differences between men and women or confuse or alter gender.

The restored Church's positions on these fundamentals frequently provoke opposition. We understand that. Our Heavenly Father's plan allows for "opposition in all things,"[18] and Satan's most strenuous opposition is directed at whatever is most important to that plan. Consequently, he seeks to oppose progress toward exaltation by distorting marriage, discouraging childbearing, or confusing gender. However, we know that in the long run, the divine purpose and plan of our loving Heavenly Father will not be changed.

Personal circumstances may change, and God's plan assures that in the long run, the faithful who keep their covenants will have the opportunity to qualify for every promised blessing.[19]

A uniquely valuable teaching to help us prepare for eternal life, "the greatest of all the gifts of God,"[20] is the 1995 proclamation on the family.[21] Its declarations are, of course, different from some current laws, practices, and advocacy, such as cohabitation and same-sex marriage. Those who do not fully understand the Father's loving plan for His children may consider this family proclamation no more than a changeable statement of policy. In contrast, we affirm that the family proclamation, founded on irrevocable doctrine, defines the kind of family relationships where the most important part of our eternal development can occur.

That is the context for the unique doctrine and policies of the restored Church of Jesus Christ of Latter-day Saints.

IV.

In many relationships and circumstances in mortal life, each of us must live with differences. As followers of Christ who should love our fellow men, we should live peacefully with those who do not believe as we do. We are all children of a loving Heavenly Father. For all of us, He has destined life after death and, ultimately, a kingdom of glory. God desires all of us to strive for His highest possible blessings by keeping His highest commandments, covenants, and ordinances, all of which culminate in His holy temples being built throughout the world. We must seek to share these truths of eternity with others. But with the love we owe to all of our neighbors, we always accept their decisions. As a Book of Mormon prophet taught, we must press forward, having "a love of God and of all men."[22]

As President Russell M. Nelson declared in our last conference: "There has never been a time in the history of the world when knowledge of our Savior is more personally vital and relevant to *every human soul*. . . . The pure doctrine of Christ is powerful. It changes the life of everyone who understands it and seeks to implement it in his or her life."[23]

May we all implement that sacred doctrine in our own lives, I pray in the name of Jesus Christ, amen.

Notes

1. See Matthew 22:36–40.
2. See Doctrine and Covenants 76:40–43.
3. John 14:2.
4. See Doctrine and Covenants 137:9.
5. See 2 Nephi 9:10–12; Doctrine and Covenants 19:4, 15, 17; 138:57–59; Bible Dictionary, "Hell."
6. Doctrine and Covenants 76:111.
7. 1 Corinthians 15:41; see also Doctrine and Covenants 76:96.
8. 1 Corinthians 15:40; see also Joseph Smith Translation (in 1 Corinthians 15:40, footnote *a*).
9. See Doctrine and Covenants 131:1.
10. See Doctrine and Covenants 76:89.
11. Doctrine and Covenants 76:43; emphasis added.
12. Doctrine and Covenants 88:36.
13. Doctrine and Covenants 88:22–24.
14. Moses 5:11; see also Doctrine and Covenants 14:7.
15. Russell M. Nelson, "Salvation and Exaltation," *Ensign* or *Liahona*, May 2008, 10.
16. See Doctrine and Covenants 131:1–3; "The Family: A Proclamation to the World," ChurchofJesusChrist.org.
17. "The Family: A Proclamation to the World," ChurchofJesusChrist.org.
18. 2 Nephi 2:11.
19. See Dallin H. Oaks, "The Great Plan of Happiness," *Ensign*, Nov. 1993, 72–75; see also *General Handbook: Serving in The Church of Jesus Christ of Latter-day Saints*, 38.1.4, ChurchofJesusChrist.org.
20. Doctrine and Covenants 14:7.
21. See "The Family: A Proclamation to the World," ChurchofJesusChrist.org.
22. 2 Nephi 31:20.
23. Russell M. Nelson, "Pure Truth, Pure Doctrine, and Pure Revelation," *Liahona*, Nov. 2021, 6.

THE COVENANT PATH: THE WAY TO ETERNAL LIFE

ELDER ADEYINKA A. OJEDIRAN
Of the Seventy

A powerful king desired for his son to rule over one of his kingdoms. The prince had to learn and grow in wisdom to sit on the throne. One day, the king met with the prince and shared his plan. They agreed the prince would go to a different town and gain experiences. He would face challenges as well as enjoy many good things there. The king then sent him to the town, where the prince was expected to prove his faithfulness to the king and demonstrate that he was fit to receive the privileges and responsibilities the king had in store for him. The prince was given the liberty to choose to receive these privileges and responsibilities or not, depending on his desires and his faithfulness. I am sure you want to know what happened to the prince. Did he return to inherit the kingdom?

Dear brothers and sisters, each of us is a prince or princess. We have been sent to mortality by a loving Heavenly Father to enjoy the blessing of a body that would become immortal through the Atonement and Resurrection of Jesus Christ. We are expected to prepare to return to God's presence by proving that we will "do all things whatsoever the Lord [our] God shall command [us]" (Abraham 3:25).

To help us, the Savior came to redeem us and show the path to return to God. God's children are invited to come to the Savior and be perfected in Him. In the scriptures, we find the invitation for us to come to the Lord repeated over 90 times, and more than half of these are personal invitations from the Lord Himself. Accepting the Savior's invitation means partaking of His ordinances and keeping our covenants with Him. Jesus Christ is "the way, the truth, and the life" (John 14:6), and He invites us "all to come unto him and partake of his goodness; and he denieth none that come unto him" (2 Nephi 26:33).

Our gospel learning and teaching deepen our conversion to

Heavenly Father and Jesus Christ and help us become more like Them. Even though not all things have been revealed concerning "the precise time and manner in which the blessings of exaltation [will be] bestowed," we are nonetheless assured of them (M. Russell Ballard, "Hope in Christ," *Liahona*, May 2021, 55).

Alma the high priest, teaching in the land of Zarahemla, recounted a profound invitation by Jesus Christ:

"Behold, he sendeth an invitation unto all men, for the arms of mercy are extended towards them, and he saith: Repent, and I will receive you.

"Yea, he saith: Come unto me and ye shall partake of the fruit of the tree of life" (Alma 5:33–34).

The Savior Himself invites us to come unto Him and take His yoke upon us that we may have rest in this tumultuous world (see Matthew 11:28–29). We come unto Christ by "exercising faith in [Him], repenting daily, making covenants with God as we receive the ordinances of salvation and exaltation, and enduring to the end by keeping those covenants" (*General Handbook: Serving in The Church of Jesus Christ of Latter-day Saints*, 1.2.1, ChurchofJesusChrist.org). The path to perfection is the covenant path, and Jesus Christ is the center of all ordinances and covenants.

King Benjamin taught that because of the covenants we make, we become sons and daughters of Christ, who has spiritually begotten us, and under His head are we made free, for "there is no other name given whereby salvation cometh" (see Mosiah 5:7–8). We are saved as we endure to the end by "following the example of the Son of the living God" (2 Nephi 31:16). Nephi counseled that all is not done by merely getting into the strait and narrow path; we "must press forward with a steadfastness in Christ, having a perfect brightness of hope, and a love of God and of all men" (see 2 Nephi 31:19–20).

The doctrine of Christ helps us find and stay on the covenant path, and the gospel is so arranged that the Lord's promised blessings are received through sacred ordinances and covenants. God's prophet, President Russell M. Nelson, admonished us in his January 16, 2018, telecast to "keep on the covenant path. Your commitment to follow the Savior by making covenants with Him and then keeping those covenants will open the door to every spiritual blessing and privilege available to men, women, and children everywhere. . . . The end for which each of us strives is to be endowed with power in a house of the Lord, sealed as families, faithful to covenants made in a temple that qualify us for the greatest gift of God—that of eternal life" ("As We Go Forward Together," *Ensign* or *Liahona*, Apr. 2018, 7).

God will not abandon His relationship with, or withhold His promised blessings of eternal life from, any faithful covenant keeper. And as we honor sacred covenants, we are drawn closer to the Savior. Elder David A. Bednar taught us yesterday that gospel covenants and ordinances operate in our lives like a compass to give us cardinal direction to come unto Christ and become more like Him.

Covenants mark the path back to God. The ordinances of baptism and receiving the gift of the Holy Ghost, priesthood ordination, and the sacrament lead us to the Lord's temple to partake of His ordinances of exaltation.

I would like to mention two things our Savior emphasized to help us faithfully keep covenants:

1. The Holy Ghost can teach us, remind us of the Savior's teachings, and abide with us forever (see John 14:16, 26). He can be our constant companion to guide us on the covenant path. President Russell M. Nelson taught that "in coming days, it will not be possible to survive spiritually without the guiding, directing, comforting, and constant influence of the Holy Ghost" ("Revelation for the Church, Revelation for Our Lives," *Ensign* or *Liahona*, May 2018, 96).

2. The Savior instituted the ordinance of the sacrament that we may always remember Him and have His Spirit to be with us. Baptism opens the gate to eternal life, and the sacrament helps us to steadfastly press forward along the covenant path. As we take the sacrament, it shall be a

testimony unto the Father that we do always remember His Son. And as we always remember Him and keep His commandments, we shall have His Spirit to be with us. Added to this promise, the Lord renews the promised remission of sin as we humbly repent of our sins.

In staying faithful to our covenants, we should endeavor to always have the Spirit to prepare us to worthily partake of the sacrament, and likewise, we regularly partake of the sacrament to always have the Spirit with us.

When our daughter was five years old, she had a battery-powered model car and loved to drive it around the house. One evening, she came to me and said, "Daddy, my car no longer drives. Could we get some gas from your car to put in it so it can drive again? Perhaps it needs gas like your car to drive."

I later observed that the battery power was down, so I said we would get it to drive in about an hour. With so much excitement, she said, "Yes! We will take it to the gas station." I simply connected the battery to an electric source to charge, and after an hour she was able to drive the car, powered by the charged battery. She thereafter learned that it is important to always recharge the battery by connecting it to an electric source.

As our daughter learned the relationship between the battery and power to drive her toy car, so we learn about Jesus Christ, the sacrament, and the Spirit. We need the Spirit to help us navigate through mortality as we faithfully keep covenants, and we need the sacrament to energize our spiritual being. Renewing our baptismal covenant and partaking of the sacrament drive faithfulness to all other covenants. A happy ending is assured as we prayerfully study and honor the Savior's invitation and enjoy His promised blessings. He said, "And that thou mayest more fully keep thyself unspotted from the world, thou shalt go to the house of prayer and offer up thy sacraments upon my holy day" (Doctrine and Covenants 59:9).

I testify that covenant keepers are promised "peace in this world, and eternal life in the world to come" (Doctrine and Covenants

59:23). I bear witness that as you regularly partake of the Savior's emblems through the sacrament, you will have His Spirit to guide you on the covenant path and stay faithful to your covenants. In the name of Jesus Christ, amen.

VALIANT DISCIPLESHIP
IN THE LATTER DAYS

ELDER JÖRG KLEBINGAT
Of the Seventy

Moral agency is God's precious gift to each of His children.[1] We are "free to choose liberty and eternal life, through the great Mediator of all men, or to choose captivity and death, according to the captivity and power of the devil."[2] God *won't* force us to do good, and the devil *can't* force us to do evil.[3] Though some may think that mortality is a contest between God and the adversary, a word from the Savior "and Satan is silenced and banished. . . . It is [our] strength that is being tested—not God's."[4]

In the end we will therefore reap what our lifelong choices have sown.[5] So what does the sum total of our thoughts, desires, words, and works say about our love for the Savior, His chosen servants, and His restored Church? Do our baptismal, priesthood, and temple covenants mean more to us than the praise of the world or the number of "likes" on social media? Is our love for the Lord and His commandments stronger than our love for anything or anyone else in this life?

The adversary and his followers have always sought to destroy the works of Christ and His prophets. The Savior's commandments, if not ignored altogether, have been rationalized into meaninglessness by many in today's world. Messengers of God who teach "inconvenient" truths are often dismissed. Even the Savior Himself was called "a man gluttonous, and a winebibber,"[6] accused of disturbing public sentiment and being divisive. Weak and conniving souls "took counsel how they might entangle him in his talk,"[7] and His "sect" of early Christians was "every where . . . spoken against."[8]

The Savior and His early followers dealt with serious internal and external opposition, and we experience the same. Today it is almost impossible to courageously live our faith without occasionally attracting a few actual and virtual fingers of scorn from the worldly. Confidently following the Savior is rewarding, but at times we may get caught in the crosshairs of those advocating an "eat, drink, and be merry"[9] philosophy, where faith in Christ, obedience, and repentance are substituted by the illusion that God will justify a little sin because He loves us so much.

Speaking "by [His] own voice or by the voice of [His] servants,"[10] did the Savior not say about our day that "the time will come when they will not endure sound doctrine; but after their own lusts shall they heap to themselves teachers" and that many "shall turn away their ears from the truth, and shall be turned unto fables"?[11] Did He not lament that "in vain they do worship me, teaching for doctrines the commandments of men"?[12] Did He not warn that "of your own selves shall men arise, speaking perverse things, to draw away disciples after them"?[13] Did He not foresee that "evil [would be called] good, and good evil"[14] and that "a man's foes shall be they of his own household"?[15]

So what about us? Should we be intimidated or afraid? Should we live our religion at periscope depth? Surely not! With faith in Christ, we need not fear the reproach of men or be afraid of their revilings.[16] With the Savior at the helm and living prophets to lead and guide us, "who can be against us?"[17] Let us be confident, not apologetic, valiant, not timid, faithful, not fearful as we hold up the Lord's light in these last days.[18]

The Savior made clear that "whosoever therefore shall confess me before men, him will I confess also before my Father. . . . But whosoever shall deny me before men, him will I also deny before my Father."[19]

Consequently, while some would prefer a God who comes without commandments, let us boldly testify, in the words of Elder D. Todd Christofferson, that "a God who makes no demands is the functional equivalent of a God who does not exist."[20]

While some would prefer to be selective in the commandments they follow, let us joyfully accept the Savior's invitation to "live by *every* word which proceedeth forth out of the mouth of God."[21]

While many believe the Lord and His Church condone doing "whatsoever [our] heart desireth,"[22] let us valiantly proclaim that it is wrong to "follow a multitude to do evil,"[23] because "crowds cannot make right what God has declared to be wrong."[24]

"O remember, remember . . . how strict [yet liberating] are the commandments of God."[25] Teaching them clearly may at times be seen as an act of intolerance. Let us therefore respectfully demonstrate that it is not only possible but essential to love a child of God who embraces beliefs different from our own.

We can accept and respect others without endorsing their beliefs or actions that do not align with the Lord's will. There is no need to sacrifice truth on the altar of agreeableness and social desirability.

Zion and Babylon are incompatible. "No man can serve two masters."[26] Let's all remember the Savior's penetrating question, "Why call ye me, Lord, Lord, and do *not* the things which I say?"[27]

Let us demonstrate our love for the Lord through wholehearted, voluntary obedience.

If you feel caught between your discipleship and the world, please remember that your loving Savior "sendeth an invitation . . . , for the arms of mercy are extended [to you], and he saith: Repent, and I will receive you."[28]

President Russell M. Nelson taught that Jesus Christ "will perform some of His mightiest works between now and when He comes again."[29] But he also taught that "those who choose the Lord's way will likely endure persecution."[30] Being "counted worthy to suffer shame for his name"[31] may at times be our lot as we "allow His voice to take priority over any other."[32]

"Blessed is he," the Savior said, "whosoever shall *not* be offended in me."[33] Elsewhere we learn that "great peace have they which *love* thy law: and *nothing* shall offend them."[34] Nothing! So let's ask ourselves, "Am I enduring for a while, but when tribulation or persecution arises because of the word, by and by am I offended?[35] Am I firmly built on the rock of Jesus Christ and His servants?"

Moral relativists advocate that truth is merely a social construct, that there are no moral absolutes. What they are really saying is that there is no sin,[36] that "whatsoever a man [does is] no crime,"[37] a philosophy for which the adversary is claiming proud authorship!

Let us therefore beware of wolves in sheep's clothing, who are always recruiting and "[often use] their intellectual reservations to cover their [own] behavioral lapses."[38]

If we really want to be valiant disciples of Christ, we will find a way. Otherwise, the adversary offers enticing alternatives. But as faithful disciples, "we need not apologize for our beliefs nor back down from that which we know to be true."[39]

In conclusion, a word about the 15 servants of God seated behind me. While the worldly "say to the seers, See not; and to the prophets, Prophesy not,"[40] the faithful are "crowned with blessings from above, yea, and with commandments not a few, and with revelations in their time."[41]

Not surprisingly, these men frequently become the lightning rods for those unhappy with the word of God as the prophets proclaim it. Those who reject the prophets don't realize that "no prophecy of the scripture is [to be] of any private interpretation" or the result of the will of man "but [that] holy men of God [speak now] as they [are] moved by the Holy Ghost."[42]

Like Paul, these men of God are "not . . . ashamed of the testimony of our Lord" and are His "prisoner[s]"[43] in the sense that the doctrine they teach is not theirs but His who called them. Like Peter, they "cannot but speak the things which [they] have seen and heard."[44] I testify that the First Presidency and the Quorum of the Twelve are good and honest men who love God and His children and who are loved by Him. Their words we should receive as if from the Lord's own mouth "in all patience and faith. For by doing these things the gates of hell shall not prevail against [us]; . . . and the Lord God will disperse the powers of darkness from before [us]."[45]

"No unhallowed hand can stop the work from progressing";[46] it will march on triumphantly with or without you or me, so "choose you this day whom ye will serve."[47] Don't be fooled or intimidated by the loud adversarial noises emanating from the great and spacious building. Their desperate decibels are no match for the serene influence of the still, small voice upon broken hearts and contrite spirits.

I testify that Christ lives, that He is our Savior and Redeemer, and that He leads His Church through the First Presidency and the Quorum of the Twelve Apostles, thus assuring that we are not "tossed to and fro, and carried about with every wind of doctrine."[48]

"True disciples of Jesus Christ," President Nelson taught, "are willing to stand out, speak up, and be different from the people of the world. They are undaunted, devoted, and courageous."[49]

Brothers and sisters, it's a good day to be good! In the sacred name of Jesus Christ, amen.

Notes

1. See Doctrine and Covenants 101:78.
2. 2 Nephi 2:27.
3. See *Teachings of Presidents of the Church: Joseph Smith* (2007), 214.
4. Hugh Nibley, "Beyond Politics," *BYU Studies*, vol. 15, no. 1 (1974), 8.
5. See 2 Corinthians 9:6; Doctrine and Covenants 6:33.
6. Matthew 11:19.
7. Matthew 22:15.
8. Acts 28:22.
9. 2 Nephi 28:7.
10. Doctrine and Covenants 1:38.
11. 2 Timothy 4:3–4.
12. Matthew 15:9.
13. Acts 20:30.
14. Isaiah 5:20.
15. Matthew 10:36.
16. See 2 Nephi 8:7.
17. Romans 8:31.
18. See 3 Nephi 18:24.
19. Matthew 10:32–33.
20. D. Todd Christofferson, "Free Forever, to Act for Themselves," *Ensign* or *Liahona*, Nov. 2014, 18.
21. Doctrine and Covenants 98:11; emphasis added.
22. Helaman 13:27.
23. Exodus 23:2.
24. Neal A. Maxwell, "Answer Me," *Ensign*, Nov. 1988, 33.
25. Alma 37:13.
26. Matthew 6:24.
27. Luke 6:46; emphasis added.
28. Alma 5:33.
29. Russell M. Nelson, "Revelation for the Church, Revelation for Our Lives," *Ensign* or *Liahona*, May 2018, 96.
30. Russell M. Nelson, "Now Is the Time to Prepare," *Ensign* or *Liahona*, May 2005, 17.
31. Acts 5:41.
32. Russell M. Nelson, "Let God Prevail," *Ensign* or *Liahona*, Nov. 2020, 94.
33. Matthew 11:6; emphasis added.
34. Psalm 119:165; emphasis added.
35. See Matthew 13:20–21.
36. See 2 Nephi 2:13.
37. Alma 30:17; see also Alma 1:4.
38. Neal A. Maxwell, "Remember How Merciful the Lord Hath Been," *Ensign* or *Liahona*, May 2004, 45; see also Neal A. Maxwell, *All These Things Shall Give Thee Experience* (1979), 110.
39. M. Russell Ballard, "How Is It with Us?," *Ensign*, May 2000, 33; *Liahona*, July 2000, 40.

40. Isaiah 30:10.
41. Doctrine and Covenants 59:4.
42. 2 Peter 1:20–21.
43. 2 Timothy 1:8.
44. Acts 4:20.
45. Doctrine and Covenants 21:5–6.
46. *Teachings: Joseph Smith*, 444.
47. Joshua 24:15.
48. Ephesians 4:14.
49. Russell M. Nelson, "Drawing the Power of Jesus Christ into Our Lives," *Ensign* or *Liahona*, May 2017, 40–41.

CONVERSION IS OUR GOAL

MARK L. PACE

Sunday School General President

For just over three years now, we have been on a journey together as members of the Lord's Church. It was October 2018 when the First Presidency and the Quorum of the Twelve Apostles invited us to learn of Jesus Christ by studying the scriptures in a new and inspiring fashion, with the *Come, Follow Me* resource as our guide.

On any journey, it's good to pause occasionally to assess our progress and to make sure we are still moving toward our goal.

Conversion Is Our Goal

Consider this profound statement from the introduction to *Come, Follow Me*:

"The aim of all gospel learning and teaching is to deepen our conversion to Heavenly Father and Jesus Christ. . . .

". . . The kind of gospel learning that strengthens our faith and leads to the miracle of conversion doesn't happen all at once. It extends beyond a classroom into our hearts and homes. It requires consistent, daily efforts to understand and live the gospel. Gospel learning that leads to true conversion requires the influence of the Holy Ghost."[1]

That is the miracle we seek—when one person has an experience in the scriptures[2] and that experience is blessed by the influence of the Holy Ghost. Such experiences are precious foundation stones for our conversion to the Savior. And as President Russell M. Nelson recently reminded us, spiritual foundations must be constantly reinforced.[3] Long-lasting conversion is a lifelong process.[4] Conversion is our goal.

To be most effective, your experiences with the scriptures must be your own.[5] Reading or hearing about another person's experiences and insights can be helpful, but that won't bring the same converting power. There is no substitute for the time *you* spend in the scriptures, hearing the Holy Ghost speak directly to *you*.

What Is the Holy Ghost Teaching Me?

Each week when I open my *Come, Follow Me* manual, I write this question at the top of the page: "What is the Holy Ghost teaching me this week as I read these chapters?"

As I study the scriptures, I ponder that question over and over again. And without fail, spiritual impressions come, and I make note of them in my manual.

Now, how do I know when the Holy Ghost is teaching me? Well, it usually happens in small and simple ways. Sometimes a passage of scripture will seem to jump off the page to my attention. At other times, I feel like my mind is enlightened with a broader understanding of a gospel principle. I also feel the influence of the Holy Ghost when my wife, Anne Marie, and I talk about what we are reading. Her perspectives always invite the Spirit.

The Prophet and the Passover

This year we are studying the Old Testament—sacred scripture that fills our souls with light. While reading the Old Testament, I feel like I am spending time with trusted guides: Adam, Eve, Enoch, Noah, Abraham, and so many others.

This week, while studying Exodus chapters 7–13, we learn how the Lord freed the children of Israel from centuries of captivity in Egypt. We read about nine plagues—nine impressive manifestations of God's power—that Pharaoh witnessed without softening his heart.

Then the Lord told His prophet, Moses, about a tenth plague—and how each family in Israel could prepare for it. As part of a ritual they would call the Passover, the Israelites were to sacrifice a male lamb, one without blemish. Then they were to mark the doorframes of their homes with the blood of the lamb. The Lord promised that all the homes that were marked with the blood would be protected from the terrible plague that was about to come.

The scriptures say, "And the children of Israel . . . did as the Lord . . . commanded Moses" (Exodus 12:28). There is something very powerful in that simple statement of obedience.

Because the children of Israel followed the counsel of Moses and acted in faith, they were saved from the plague and, in time, freed from their captivity.

So what did the Holy Ghost teach me in these chapters this week?

Here are a few thoughts that have rested on my mind:

- The Lord works through His prophet to protect and save His people.
- The faith and humility to follow the prophet preceded the miracle of protection and deliverance.
- The blood on the doorframe was an outward sign of inward faith in Jesus Christ, the Lamb of God.

The Prophet and the Lord's Promises

I am impressed with the parallel between the way the Lord blessed His people in this Old Testament account and the way He is also blessing His people today.

When the Lord's living prophet, President Nelson, introduced us to *Come, Follow Me* as a means of studying the scriptures, he invited us to transform our homes into sanctuaries of faith and centers of gospel learning.

Then he promised four specific blessings:

1. *your* Sabbath days will be a delight,
2. *your* children will be excited to learn and live the Savior's teachings,
3. the influence of the adversary in *your* life and in *your* home will decrease, and
4. these changes in *your* family will be dramatic and sustaining.[6]

Now, we don't have any journal entries from those who experienced the Passover with Moses in Egypt. However, we do have many testimonials from Saints who, with equal faith, are following President Nelson's counsel today and receiving the promised blessings.

Here are a few such testimonials:

A mother of a young family said: "We talk of Christ and rejoice in Christ in our home. To me that is the greatest blessing—that my children can grow up with these gospel conversations in the home that bring them closer to the Savior."[7]

A senior brother called his study of the scriptures through *Come, Follow Me* "a conduit filled with divine light that helps us see gospel doctrine that is necessary for our spiritual well-being."[8]

A young wife described the blessings in her marriage: "I have been able to know my husband's heart more deeply, and I have been able to open my heart more to him as we study together."[9]

A mother of a large family noticed how her efforts to teach her family changed. She mentioned: "Looking back, it was like I was playing the piano with snow gloves on. I was going through the motions, but the music wasn't quite right. Now the gloves are off, and while my music still isn't perfect, I hear the difference. *Come, Follow Me* has given me vision, ability, focus, and purpose."[10]

A young husband said: "My most important priorities at home have become more clear since I've made *Come, Follow Me* a regular part of my mornings. Studying leads me to think more about the things that matter most to me, like the temple, my relationship with my wife, and my calling. I'm grateful that my home is a sanctuary where God comes first."[11]

A sister shared: "My daily experiences with *Come, Follow Me* are rarely noteworthy, but over time I can see how I am being changed by such a constant, focused study of the scriptures. That kind of study humbles me, teaches me, and changes me a little at a time."[12]

A returned missionary reported: "The *Come, Follow Me* program has gotten me closer to the level of scripture study that I did on my mission, and I have been able to move from a checklist mentality of scripture study to truly enriching sessions of getting to know God."[13]

A brother said: "I feel the Holy Ghost welcomed more into my life and feel God's revelatory guidance in making decisions. I have more profound conversations regarding the beauty in the simple doctrine of Christ and His Atonement."[14]

A seven-year-old child shared: "I'm getting baptized soon, and *Come, Follow Me* is getting me ready. My family and I talk about baptism, and I don't feel nervous about getting baptized now. *Come, Follow Me* helps the Holy Ghost come into my heart, and I feel warm when I read the scriptures."[15]

And then finally, from a mother of several children: "As we study the word of God, He has helped our family move from concern to power; from trial and challenge to deliverance; from contention and criticism to love and peace; and from the adversary's influence to God's influence."[16]

These and many other faithful followers of Christ have symbolically placed the blood of the Lamb of God on the entrance to their homes. They are demonstrating their inward commitment to follow the Savior. Their faith precedes the miracle. It is the miracle of one person having an experience in the scriptures and that experience being blessed by the influence of the Holy Ghost.

When we study the scriptures, there is no spiritual famine in the land. As Nephi said, "Whoso would hearken unto the word of God, and would hold fast unto it, they would never perish; neither could the temptations and the fiery darts of the adversary overpower them unto blindness, to lead them away to destruction" (1 Nephi 15:24).

In ancient times, as the children of Israel followed the Lord's direction given through the prophet Moses, they were blessed with safety and freedom. Today, as we follow the Lord's direction given through our living prophet, President Nelson, we are equally blessed with conversion in our hearts and protection in our homes.

I testify that Jesus Christ lives. This is His Church, restored to the earth through the Prophet Joseph Smith. President Russell M. Nelson is the Lord's prophet today. I love and sustain him. In the name of Jesus Christ, amen.

Notes

1. *Come, Follow Me—For Individuals and Families: Old Testament 2022*, vii.
2. "We are each responsible for our individual spiritual growth" (Russell M. Nelson, "Opening Remarks," *Ensign* or *Liahona*, Nov. 2018, 8).
3. See Russell M. Nelson, "The Temple and Your Spiritual Foundation," *Liahona*, Nov. 2021, 93–96.

4. This is an important reason why President Nelson has pleaded with us to "make time for the Lord! Make your own spiritual foundation firm and able to stand the test of time by doing those things that allow the Holy Ghost to be with you *always*" ("Make Time for the Lord," *Liahona*, Nov. 2021, 120).

5. "Regardless of what others may say or do, no one can ever take away a witness borne to your heart and mind about what is true" (Russell M. Nelson, "Revelation for the Church, Revelation for Our Lives," *Ensign* or *Liahona*, May 2018, 95).

6. See Russell M. Nelson, "Becoming Exemplary Latter-day Saints," *Ensign* or *Liahona*, Nov. 2018, 113–14. President Nelson repeated this invitation last April: "Your commitment to make your home your *primary* sanctuary of faith should *never* end. As faith and holiness decrease in this fallen world, your need for holy places will increase. I urge you to continue to make your home a truly holy place 'and *be not moved*' [Doctrine and Covenants 87:8; emphasis added] from that essential goal" ("What We Are Learning and Will Never Forget," *Liahona*, May 2021, 79).

7. Personal correspondence; see also 2 Nephi 25:26.

8. Personal correspondence.

9. Personal correspondence.

10. Personal correspondence.

11. Personal correspondence.

12. Personal correspondence.

13. Personal correspondence.

14. Personal correspondence.

15. Personal correspondence.

16. Personal correspondence.

IN AWE OF CHRIST AND HIS GOSPEL

ELDER ULISSES SOARES
Of the Quorum of the Twelve Apostles

I have a dear friend who is a brilliant, retired university professor, a prolific author, and, above all, a committed disciple of Jesus Christ. He has visited the Holy Land dozens of times to participate in conferences, conduct academic research, and lead tours. According to him, every time he visits the land where Jesus walked, he marvels because he undoubtedly learns something new, astonishing, and fascinating about the Savior, His mortal ministry, and His beloved homeland. The awe my friend shows when he talks about all that he learns in the Holy Land is contagious, and this amazement has been fundamental in his great achievements and academic pursuits in his life.

As I have listened to his experiences and felt of his enthusiasm, I have reflected on how much more spiritual wonder, so to speak, that we can and should feel for the gospel of Jesus Christ and the difference it can make in our discipleship and in our journey toward eternal life. The wonder I refer to is the sensation of emotion, awe, or amazement common to all who wholeheartedly center their lives on the Savior and His teachings and humbly recognize His presence in their lives. Such a feeling of wonder, inspired by the influence of the Holy Ghost, stimulates the enthusiasm to joyfully live the doctrine of Christ.[1]

The scriptures contain several examples of how this sensation is manifest. The prophet Isaiah, for example, expressed the depth of his gratitude for the Lord through his rejoicing in Him.[2] Those who heard Jesus preaching in the synagogue at Capernaum were astonished at His doctrine and the strength with which He taught.[3] It was this same feeling that penetrated every fiber of young Joseph Smith's heart as he read from the Bible the first chapter of James, leading him to seek the wisdom of God.[4]

My brothers and sisters, when we truly are in awe of Jesus Christ and His gospel, we are happier, we have more enthusiasm for God's work, and we recognize the Lord's hand in all things. Additionally, our study of God's words is more meaningful; our prayers, more intentional; our worship, more reverent; our service in God's kingdom, more diligent. All these actions contribute to the Holy Spirit's influence being more frequent in our lives.[5] Thus, our testimony of the Savior and His gospel will be strengthened, we will keep Christ alive in us,[6] and we will live our lives "rooted and built up in him, and stablished in the faith, . . . abounding therein with thanksgiving."[7] When we live in this way, we become more spiritually resilient and protected against falling into the trap of spiritual apathy.

Such apathy is characterized by the gradual loss of our excitement to engage fully in the Lord's gospel. It generally begins when we are feeling that we have already attained all the necessary knowledge and blessings for our happiness in this life. This complacency, so to speak, causes us to take the gospel gifts for granted, and from then on, we run the risk of neglecting both our regular immersion in the essentials of the gospel of Jesus Christ[8] and the covenants we have made. Consequently, we gradually distance ourselves from the Lord, weakening our ability to "hear Him,"[9] becoming indifferent and insensitive to the greatness of His work. Doubt regarding the truths we have already received may enter our mind and heart, making us vulnerable to the enemy's temptations.[10]

Pastor Aiden Wilson Tozer, a renowned writer and valiant Christian, wrote, "Complacency is a deadly foe of all spiritual growth."[11] Wasn't this exactly what happened to the people of Nephi shortly after the birth of Christ? They "began to be less and less astonished at a sign or a wonder from heaven, . . . [disbelieving] all which they had heard and seen." Thus did Satan "blind their eyes and lead them away to believe that the doctrine of Christ was a foolish and a vain thing."[12]

My beloved brothers and sisters, in His perfect and infinite love and knowing our human nature,[13] the Savior has established the way for us to avoid falling into the trap of spiritual apathy. The Savior's invitation gives us a broader perspective, especially considering the complex world in which we live: "Learn of me, and listen to my words; walk in the meekness of my Spirit, and you shall have peace in me."[14] As we accept the Savior's invitation, we demonstrate our humility, our desire to be teachable, and our hope to become more like Him.[15] This invitation also includes serving Him and ministering to God's children "with all [our] heart, might, mind and strength."[16] At the core of our effort in this journey are, of course, the two great commandments: to love the Lord our God and love our neighbor as ourselves.[17]

This type of behavior is part of Jesus's divine character and was evident in everything He did during His earthly ministry.[18] Therefore, when we intentionally and truly dedicate ourselves to look unto Him and learn from His perfect example,[19] we come to know Him better. We grow in enthusiasm and desire to incorporate into our lives the ultimate standard of how we should live, the example we should set, and the commandments we should follow. We also gain additional understanding, wisdom, divine character, and grace toward God and our neighbors.[20] I can assure you that our ability to feel the Savior's influence and love will be intensified in our lives, magnifying our faith, our desire to act righteously, and the motivation to serve Him and others.[21] In addition, our gratitude for the blessings and challenges we experience in mortality will solidify and become part of our true worship.[22]

My dear friends, all these things strengthen our spiritual wonder regarding the gospel and move us to joyfully keep the covenants we make with the Lord—even in the midst of the trials and challenges we experience. Of course, for these outcomes to happen, we need to immerse ourselves with faith and real intent in the Savior's teachings,[23] striving to incorporate His attributes into our way of being.[24] In addition, we need to draw nearer to Him through our repentance,[25] seeking His forgiveness and His redeeming power in our lives and keeping His commandments. The Lord Himself promised that He would direct our paths if we would trust in Him with all our hearts, acknowledging Him in all our ways and not leaning on our own understanding.[26]

A man I met recently, whose name is Wes and who is attending the conference today, accepted Christ's invitation to learn of Him and of His gospel and began to experience the awe of His love after 27 years of distancing himself from the covenant path. He told me that one day he was contacted via Facebook by a missionary, Elder Jones, who was temporarily assigned to Wes's area before going to his originally assigned mission in Panama. When Elder Jones came across Wes's profile, not even knowing beforehand that he was already a member of the Church, he felt the guidance of the Holy Ghost and knew that he should immediately contact Wes. He quickly acted on this impression. Wes was amazed by this unexpected contact and began to realize that the Lord was aware of him despite his distance from the covenant path.

From then on, Wes and the missionaries began to communicate frequently. Elder Jones and his companion provided weekly acts of service and spiritual messages that helped Wes to recover his awe of the Savior and His gospel. It rekindled the flame of his testimony of the truth and of the Savior's love for him. Wes felt the peace that comes from the Comforter and gained the strength he needed to return to the fold. He told me that this experience brought him spiritually and emotionally back to life and helped him to eliminate the feelings of bitterness accumulated over the years because of the difficult experiences he had been through.

As my aforementioned thoughtful professor friend has observed, there is always something wonderful and fascinating to learn about Jesus Christ and His gospel.[27] The Lord has made wonderful promises that are extended to all those, including us, who seek to learn of Him and incorporate His words into their lives. To Enoch, He said, "Behold my Spirit [shall be] upon you, wherefore all thy words will I justify; and the mountains shall flee before you, and the rivers shall turn from their course; and thou shalt abide in me, and I in you."[28] Through His servant King Benjamin, He declared, "Ye shall be called the children of Christ, his sons, and his daughters; for behold, this day he hath spiritually begotten you; for ye say that your

175

hearts are changed through faith on his name; therefore, ye are born of him and have become his sons and his daughters."[29]

Therefore, as we genuinely and continually strive to learn of the Savior and follow His example, I promise you, in His name, that His divine attributes will be written in our minds and hearts,[30] that we will become more like Him, and that we will walk with Him.[31]

My beloved brothers and sisters, I pray that we will ever stand in awe of Jesus Christ and His complete, infinite, and perfect love. May the remembrance of what our eyes have seen and our hearts have felt increase our amazement at the Savior's atoning sacrifice, which can heal us of our spiritual and emotional wounds and help us to draw closer to Him. May we marvel at the great promises that the Father has in His hands and that He has prepared for those who are faithful:

"The kingdom is yours and the blessings thereof are yours, and the riches of eternity are yours.

"And he who receiveth all things with thankfulness shall be made glorious."[32]

Jesus is the Redeemer of the world, and this is His Church. I bear witness of these truths in the awe-inspiring, sacred, and sublime name of our Savior, Jesus Christ, amen.

Notes

1. See Guide to the Scriptures, "Doctrine of Christ," scriptures.ChurchofJesusChrist.org.
2. See Isaiah 61:10.
3. See Mark 1:22.
4. See Joseph Smith—History 1:11–13.
5. See Guide to the Scriptures, "Holy Ghost," scriptures.ChurchofJesusChrist.org.
6. See Galatians 2:20.
7. Colossians 2:7; see verses 6–8.
8. See Matthew 14:23; 1 Nephi 19:23; Helaman 3:35; 4 Nephi 1:12; Russell M. Nelson, "Becoming Exemplary Latter-day Saints," *Ensign* or *Liahona*, Nov. 2018, 113–14.
9. See Matthew 17:5; Luke 9:35; 3 Nephi 11:7.
10. See 1 Peter 5:8.
11. A. W. Tozer, *The Pursuit of God* (2015), 23.
12. 3 Nephi 2:1–2.
13. See Guide to the Scriptures, "Natural Man," scriptures.ChurchofJesusChrist.org.
14. Doctrine and Covenants 19:23.
15. See Guide to the Scriptures, "Humble, Humility," scriptures.ChurchofJesusChrist.org.
16. Doctrine and Covenants 4:2.
17. See Matthew 22:36–40.
18. See Guide to the Scriptures, "Jesus Christ," scriptures.ChurchofJesusChrist.org.
19. See Doctrine and Covenants 6:36.

20. See Luke 2:52.
21. See Guide to the Scriptures, "Righteous, Righteousness," scriptures.ChurchofJesusChrist.org.
22. See Guide to the Scriptures, "Thankful, Thanks, Thanksgiving," scriptures.ChurchofJesusChrist .org.
23. See 2 Nephi 32:3.
24. See *Preach My Gospel: A Guide to Missionary Service* (2019), 121–32.
25. See Russell M. Nelson, "We Can Do Better and Be Better," *Ensign* or *Liahona*, May 2019, 67–69.
26. See Doctrine and Covenants 11:12–14; see also Proverbs 3:5–6.
27. See Doctrine and Covenants 89:19; 121:42; 130:19.
28. Moses 6:34.
29. Mosiah 5:7.
30. See 2 Corinthians 3:3.
31. See Guide to the Scriptures, "Walk, Walk with God," scriptures.ChurchofJesusChrist.org.
32. Doctrine and Covenants 78:18–19.

COME INTO THE FOLD OF GOD

ELDER RANDY D. FUNK
Of the Seventy

As young parents, Brother and Sister Samad learned the gospel of Jesus Christ in their simple two-room home in Semarang, Indonesia.[1] Seated around a small table, with a dim light that seemed to provide more mosquitoes than illumination, two young missionaries taught them eternal truths. Through sincere prayer and the guidance of the Holy Ghost, they came to believe what they were taught and chose to be baptized and become members of The Church of Jesus Christ of Latter-day Saints. That decision, and their pattern of living since, has blessed Brother and Sister Samad and their family in every aspect of their lives.[2]

They are among the early pioneer Saints in Indonesia. Later they received the ordinances of the temple, and Brother Samad served as the branch president and then district president, driving throughout Central Java to fulfill his responsibilities. For the past decade, he has served as the first patriarch of the Surakarta Indonesia Stake.

As one of the missionaries in that humble, faith-filled home 49 years ago, I have witnessed in them what King Benjamin taught in the Book of Mormon: "I would desire that ye should consider on the blessed and happy state of those that keep the commandments of God. For behold, they are blessed in all things, both temporal and spiritual."[3] The blessings that flow into the lives of those who follow the example and teachings of Jesus Christ, who choose to be counted among His disciples, are numerous, joyful, and eternal.[4]

The Fold of God

Alma's baptismal covenant invitation to those gathered at the Waters of Mormon begins with this phrase: "Now, as ye are desirous to come into the fold of God."[5]

A fold, or sheepfold, is a large enclosure, often constructed with stone walls, where the sheep are protected at night. It has only one opening. At the end of the day, the shepherd calls the sheep. They know his voice, and through the gate they enter the safety of the fold.

The people of Alma would have known that shepherds stand at the narrow opening of the fold so that when the sheep enter, they are numbered[6] and their wounds and ailments noted and cared for one by one. The safety and well-being of the sheep depend on their willingness to come into the fold and to stay in the fold.

Among us there may be some who feel they are at the edge of the flock, perhaps thinking they are less needed or valued or that they don't belong in the fold. And, as in the sheepfold, in the fold of God we sometimes step on one another's toes and need to repent or forgive.

But the Good Shepherd[7]—our true shepherd—is always good. Within the fold of God, we experience His watchful, nurturing care and are blessed to feel His redeeming love. He said, "I have graven thee upon the palms of my hands; thy walls are continually before me."[8] Our Savior has graven upon His palms our sins, pains, afflictions,[9] and all that is unfair in life.[10] All are welcome to receive these blessings, as they "are desirous to come"[11] and choose to be in the fold. The gift of agency is not simply the right to choose; it is the opportunity to choose the right. And the walls of the fold are not a constraint but a source of spiritual safety.

Jesus taught that there is "one fold, and one shepherd."[12] He said:

"He that entereth in by the door is the shepherd of the sheep. . . .

"And the sheep hear his voice . . . ,

". . . and the sheep follow him: for they know his voice."[13]

Jesus then stated, "I am the door: by me if any man enter in, he shall be saved,"[14] teaching clearly that there is only one way into the fold of God and only one way to be saved. It is by and through Jesus Christ.[15]

Blessings Come to Those in the Fold of God

We learn how to come into the fold from the word of God, which is the doctrine taught by Jesus Christ and His prophets.[16] When we follow the doctrine of Christ and come into the fold through faith in Jesus Christ, repentance, baptism and confirmation, and continuing faithfulness,[17] Alma promised four specific, personal blessings. *You* may (1) "be redeemed of God," (2) "be numbered with those of the first resurrection," (3) "have eternal life," and (4) the Lord will "pour out his Spirit more abundantly upon you."[18]

After Alma taught about these blessings, the people clapped their hands for joy. Here's why:

First: To *redeem* means to pay off a debt or obligation or to free from what distresses or harms.[19] No amount of personal improvement on our part can make us clean from the sins we have committed or whole from the wounds we have suffered without the Atonement of Jesus Christ. He is our Redeemer.[20]

Second: Because of Christ's Resurrection, all will be resurrected.[21] After our spirits depart our mortal bodies, we will undoubtedly look forward to when we can again with a resurrected body embrace those we love. We will eagerly look forward to being among those of the First Resurrection.

Third: Eternal life means to live with God and as He lives. It is "the greatest of all the gifts of God"[22] and will bring a fulness of joy.[23] It is the ultimate purpose and objective of our lives.

Fourth: The companionship of a member of the Godhead, the Holy Ghost, provides much-needed guidance and comfort during this mortal life.[24]

Consider some causes of unhappiness: misery comes from sin,[25] sadness and loneliness from the death of a loved one, and fear from the uncertainty of what happens when we die. But when we enter the fold of God and keep our covenants with Him, we feel the peace of knowing and trusting that Christ will redeem us from our sins, that the separation of our body and spirit will end more quickly, and that we will live eternally with God in a most glorious manner.

Trust in Christ and Act in Faith

Brothers and sisters, the scriptures are filled with examples of the Savior's majestic power and His compassionate mercy and grace. During His earthly ministry, His blessings of healing came to those who trusted Him and acted in faith. For example, the infirm man at the pool of Bethesda walked when, with faith, he followed the Savior's command to "rise, take up thy bed, and walk."[26] Those who were sick or afflicted in any manner in the land of Bountiful were healed when "with one accord" they "did go forth."[27]

Similarly, to receive the marvelous blessings promised to those who come into the fold of God requires us to do just that—we need to choose to come. Alma the Younger taught, "And now I say unto you that the good shepherd doth call after you; and if you will hearken unto his voice he will bring you into his fold."[28]

Several years ago a dear friend passed away from cancer. When his wife, Sharon, first wrote about his diagnosis, she said: "We Choose Faith. Faith in our Savior, Jesus Christ. Faith in our Heavenly Father's plan, and faith that He knows our needs and fulfills His promises."[29]

I have met many Latter-day Saints like Sharon who feel the inward peace of being securely within the fold of God, especially when temptation, opposition, or adversity comes.[30] They have chosen to have faith in Jesus Christ and to follow His prophet. Our dear prophet, President Russell M. Nelson, has taught, "Everything good in life—every potential blessing of eternal significance—begins with faith."[31]

Come Fully into the Fold of God

My great-great-great-grandfather James Sawyer Holman came to Utah in 1847, but he wasn't among those to arrive in July with Brigham Young. He came later that year and, according to family records, was responsible to bring the sheep. He didn't reach the Salt Lake Valley until October, but he and the sheep made it.[32]

Figuratively speaking, some of us are still on the plains. Not everyone arrives in the first group. My dear friends, please continue the journey—and help others—to come fully into the fold of God. The blessings of the gospel of Jesus Christ are immeasurable because they are eternal.

I am profoundly grateful to be a member of The Church of Jesus Christ of Latter-day Saints. I bear witness of the love of our

Heavenly Father and our Redeemer, Jesus Christ, and of the peace that comes only from Them—the inner peace and the blessings found in the fold of God. In the name of Jesus Christ, amen.

Notes

1. Like many Indonesians of his generation, Brother Samad has just one name. His wife, Sri Katoningsih, and their children use Samad as their surname.
2. Brother and Sister Samad report that at least 44 of their extended family are now members of the Church. Many others also enjoy the blessings of the gospel because of their example and service.
3. Mosiah 2:41.
4. See Doctrine and Covenants 59:23.
5. Mosiah 18:8.
6. See Moroni 6:4.
7. See John 10:14; see also Gerrit W. Gong, "Good Shepherd, Lamb of God," *Ensign* or *Liahona*, May 2019, 97–101.
8. Isaiah 49:16.
9. See Alma 7:11–13.
10. See Dale G. Renlund, "Infuriating Unfairness," *Ensign* or *Liahona*, May 2021, 41–44.
11. Mosiah 18:8.
12. John 10:16.
13. John 10:2–4.
14. John 10:9.
15. See 2 Nephi 31:21; Helaman 5:9.
16. See Henry B. Eyring, "The Power of Teaching Doctrine," *Ensign*, May 1999, 73; *Liahona*, July 1999, 85. When we seek to come unto Christ, we must come according to the words of Christ, "for there is one God and one Shepherd over all the earth" (see 1 Nephi 13:40–41).
17. The doctrine of Christ, simply stated, is that all people everywhere must exercise faith in Jesus Christ and His Atonement, repent, be baptized, receive the Holy Ghost, and endure to the end, or, as the Savior taught in 3 Nephi 11:38, "ye can in nowise inherit the kingdom of God."
18. Mosiah 18:9, 10.
19. See *Merriam-Webster.com Dictionary*, "redeem"; see also D. Todd Christofferson, "Redemption," *Ensign* or *Liahona*, May 2013, 109.
20. See Alma 11:40.
21. See 2 Nephi 2:8; 9:12.
22. Doctrine and Covenants 14:7.
23. See 2 Nephi 9:18.
24. See 1 Nephi 4:6; Moroni 8:26.
25. See Mosiah 3:24–25; Alma 41:10.
26. John 5:8.
27. 3 Nephi 17:9.
28. Alma 5:60. In Moses 7:53, the Messiah also said, "Whoso cometh in at the gate and climbeth up by me shall never fall."
29. Sharon Jones, "Diagnosis," wechoosefaith.blogspot.com, Mar. 18, 2012.
30. *Preach My Gospel* defines "endure to the end" as follows: "To remain true to the commandments of God and be true to the endowment and sealing ordinances of the temple despite temptation, opposition, and adversity throughout life" ([2019], 73). This suggests that we will experience temptation, opposition, and adversity throughout life.
31. Russell M. Nelson, "Christ Is Risen; Faith in Him Will Move Mountains," *Ensign* or *Liahona*, May 2021, 102.
32. See brief biographies of James Sawyer Holman and Naomi Roxina LeBaron Holman by their granddaughter Grace H. Sainsbury in the possession of the speaker (Charles C. Rich diary, Sept. 28, 1847, Church History Library, Salt Lake City; Journal History of The Church of Jesus Christ of Latter-day Saints, June 21, 1847, 49, Church History Library). Holman was a captain in the 1847 Charles C. Rich company.

OUR HEARTFELT ALL

ELDER DIETER F. UCHTDORF
Of the Quorum of the Twelve Apostles

An Offering unto Him

Just days before He gave His life for us, Jesus Christ was at the temple in Jerusalem, watching people make donations to the temple treasury. "Many that were rich cast in much," but then, along came a poor widow, "and she threw in two mites." It was such a small amount, it would hardly be worth recording.

And yet this seemingly inconsequential donation caught the Savior's attention. In fact, it impressed Him so deeply that "he called unto him his disciples, and saith unto them, Verily I say unto you, That this poor widow hath cast more in, than all they which have cast into the treasury:

"For all they did cast in of their abundance; but she of her want did cast in all that she had, even all her living."[1]

With this simple observation, the Savior taught us how offerings are measured in His kingdom—and it's quite different from the way we usually measure things. To the Lord, the value of the donation was measured not by the effect it had on the treasury but by the effect it had on the heart of the donor.

In praising this faithful widow, the Savior gave us a standard to measure our discipleship in all of its many expressions. Jesus taught that our offering may be large or it may be small, but either way, it must be our heartfelt *all*.

This principle is echoed in the plea of the Book of Mormon prophet Amaleki: "Come unto Christ, who is the Holy One of Israel, and partake of his salvation, and the power of his redemption. Yea, come unto him, and offer your whole souls as an offering unto him."[2]

But how is this possible? To many of us, such a standard of whole-souled commitment seems out of reach. We are already stretched so thin. How can we balance the many demands of life with our desires to offer our whole souls to the Lord?

Perhaps our challenge is that we think balance means dividing our time evenly among competing interests. Viewed in this way, our commitment to Jesus Christ would be one of many things we need to fit into our busy schedules. But perhaps there is another way to look at it.

Balance: Like Riding a Bicycle

My wife, Harriet, and I love to go bicycle riding together. It's a wonderful way to get some exercise while also spending time together. While we're riding, and I'm not huffing and puffing too much, we enjoy the beautiful world around us and even engage in a pleasant conversation. Rarely do we have to pay much attention to keeping our balance on our bicycles. We've been riding long enough that we don't even think about that—it has become normal and natural for us.

But whenever I watch someone learning to ride a bike for the first time, I'm reminded that it's not easy balancing yourself on those two narrow wheels. It takes time. It takes practice. It takes patience. It even takes falling down a time or two.

Most of all, those who succeed in balancing on a bicycle learn these important tips:

Don't look at your feet.

Look ahead.

Keep your eyes on the road in front of you. Focus on your destination. And get pedaling. Staying balanced is all about moving forward.

Similar principles apply when it comes to finding balance in our lives as disciples of Jesus Christ. How to distribute your time and energy among your many important tasks will vary from person to person and from one season of life to another. But our common, overall objective is to follow the Way of our Master, Jesus Christ, and return to the presence of our beloved Father in Heaven. This objective must remain constant and consistent, whoever we are and whatever else is happening in our lives.[3]

Lift: Like Flying an Airplane

Now, for those who are avid bicyclists, comparing discipleship to riding a bike may be a helpful analogy. For those who are not, don't worry. I have another analogy I'm sure every man, woman, and child will be able to relate to.

Discipleship, like most things in life, can also be compared to flying an airplane.

Have you ever stopped to think how amazing it is that a huge passenger jet can actually get off the ground and fly? What is it that keeps these flying machines soaring elegantly through the sky, crossing oceans and continents?

Put simply, an aircraft flies only when air is moving over its wings. That movement creates differences in air pressure that give the plane lift. And how do you get enough air moving over the wings to create lift? The answer is forward thrust.

The airplane gains no altitude sitting on the runway. Even on a windy day, enough lift isn't created unless the airplane is moving forward, with enough thrust to counteract the forces holding it back.

Just as forward momentum keeps a bicycle balanced and upright, moving forward helps an aircraft overcome the pull of gravity and drag.

What does this mean for us as disciples of Jesus Christ? It means that if we want to find balance in life, and if we want the Savior to lift us heavenward, then our commitment to Him and His gospel can't be casual or occasional. Like the widow at Jerusalem, we must offer Him our whole souls. Our offering may be small, but it must come from our heart and soul.

Being a disciple of Jesus Christ is not just one of many things we do. The Savior is the motivating power behind *all* that we do. He is not a rest stop in our journey. He is not a scenic byway or even a major landmark. He is "the way, the truth, and the life: no man cometh unto the Father, but by [Jesus Christ]."[4] That is the Way and our ultimate destination.

Balance and lift come as we "press forward with a steadfastness in Christ, having a perfect brightness of hope, and a love of God and of all men."[5]

Sacrifice and Consecration

And what about the many tasks and responsibilities that make our lives so busy? Spending time with loved ones, going to school or preparing for an occupation, earning a living, caring for family, serving in the community—where does it all fit in? The Savior reassures us:

"Your heavenly Father knoweth that ye have need of all these things.

"But seek ye first the kingdom of God and his righteousness, and all these things shall be added unto you."[6]

But that doesn't mean it's easy.[7] It requires both *sacrifice* and *consecration.*

It requires letting some things *go* and letting other things *grow.*

Sacrifice and consecration are two heavenly laws that we covenant to obey in the holy temple. These two laws are similar but not identical. To *sacrifice* means to give something up in favor of something more valuable. Anciently, God's people sacrificed the firstlings of their flocks in honor of the coming Messiah. Throughout history, faithful Saints have sacrificed personal desires, comforts, and even their lives for the Savior.

We all have things, large and small, we need to sacrifice in order to follow Jesus Christ more completely.[8] Our sacrifices show what we truly value. Sacrifices are sacred and honored by the Lord.[9]

Consecration is different from sacrifice in at least one important way. When we consecrate something, we don't leave it to be consumed upon the altar. Rather, we put it to use in the Lord's service. We dedicate it to Him and His holy purposes.[10] We receive the talents that the Lord has given us and strive to increase them, manifold, to become even more helpful in building the Lord's kingdom.[11]

Very few of us will ever be asked to *sacrifice* our lives for the Savior. But we are all invited to *consecrate* our lives to Him.

One Work, One Joy, One Purpose

As we seek to purify our lives and look unto Christ in every thought,[12] everything else begins to align. Life no longer feels like a long list of separate efforts held in tenuous balance.

Over time, it all becomes one work.

One joy.

One holy purpose.

It is the work of loving and serving God. It is loving and serving God's children.[13]

When we look at our lives and see a hundred things to do, we feel overwhelmed. When we see one thing—loving and serving God and His children, in a hundred different ways—then we can work on those things with joy.

This is how we offer our whole souls—by sacrificing anything that's holding us back and consecrating the rest to the Lord and His purposes.

A Word of Encouragement and Testimony

My dear brothers and sisters and my dear friends, there will be times when you wish you could do more. Your loving Father in Heaven knows your heart. He knows that you can't do everything your heart wants you to do. But you can love and serve God. You can do your best to keep His commandments. You can love and serve His children. And your efforts are purifying your heart and preparing you for a glorious future.

This is what the widow at the temple treasury seemed to understand. She surely knew that her offering would not change the fortunes of Israel, but it could change and bless *her*—because, though small, it was her all.

So, my dear friends and beloved fellow disciples of Jesus Christ, let us not be "weary in well-doing, for [we] are laying the foundation of a great work." And out of our small things will proceed "that which is great."[14]

I testify that this is true, as I also testify that Jesus Christ is our Master, our Redeemer, and our one and only Way back to our beloved Father in Heaven. In the sacred name of Jesus Christ, amen.

Notes

1. Mark 12:41–44.
2. Omni 1:26.
3. Our children and youth are invited to grow in a balanced way as they follow Jesus Christ, who as a young man "increased in wisdom and stature, and in favour with God and man" (Luke 2:52).
4. John 14:6.
5. 2 Nephi 31:20.
6. 3 Nephi 13:32–33; see also Matthew 6:32–33. Joseph Smith Translation, Matthew 6:38 provides additional insight: "Seek not the things of this world but seek ye first to build up the kingdom of God, and to establish his righteousness" (in Matthew 6:33, footnote *a*).
7. One example comes from our prophet, President Russell M. Nelson. When he was at the height of his professional career as a heart surgeon, he was called as stake president. Elders Spencer W. Kimball and LeGrand Richards extended the call. Recognizing the demands of his professional life, they said to him, "If you feel that you are too busy and shouldn't accept the call, then that's your privilege." He answered that his decision about whether or not to serve when called was made long ago, when he and his wife made temple covenants with the Lord. "We made a commitment then," he said, "to 'seek . . . first the kingdom of God, and his righteousness' [Matthew 6:33], feeling confident that everything else would be added unto us, as the Lord promised" (Russell Marion Nelson, *From Heart to Heart: An Autobiography* [1979], 114).
8. President Nelson recently spoke of "the need for each of us to remove, with the Savior's help, the old debris in our lives. . . . I invite you to pray," he said, "to identify the debris you should remove from your life so you can become more worthy" ("Welcome Message," *Liahona*, May 2021, 7).
9. The scriptures say that, to God, our sacrifices are more sacred than our accomplishments (see Doctrine and Covenants 117:13). This may be one reason the Lord valued the widow's mites more than the contribution of the wealthy. The former was a sacrifice, which has a purifying effect on the giver. The latter, while it may have accomplished more monetarily, was not a sacrifice, and it left the giver unchanged.
10. Very few of us will ever be asked to *sacrifice* our lives for the Savior. But we are all invited to *consecrate* our lives to Him.
11. See Matthew 25:14–30.
12. See Doctrine and Covenants 6:36.
13. In this way, we see in our lives a fulfillment of the prophecy of the Apostle Paul: "In the dispensation of the fulness of times [God will] gather together in one all things in Christ, both which are in heaven, and which are on earth: even in him" (Ephesians 1:10).
14. Doctrine and Covenants 64:33.

NOW IS THE TIME

PRESIDENT RUSSELL M. NELSON

President of The Church of Jesus Christ of Latter-day Saints

My dear brothers and sisters, this conference has been historic in many ways. We have been blessed by the prayers, messages, and music. We have been inspired by servants of the Lord.

We have received important direction for the future. My prayer is that the Spirit has spoken to you directly about things the Lord would have *you* do.

The future is always uncertain. Weather changes. Economic cycles are unpredictable. Disasters, accidents, and illness can change life quickly. These actions are largely beyond our control. But there are some things we *can* control, including how we spend our time each day.

I like this poem by Henry Van Dyke, posted on a sundial at Wells College in New York. It reads:

> *The shadow by my finger cast*
> *Divides the future from the past:*
> *Before it, sleeps the unborn hour*
> *In darkness, and beyond thy power:*
> *Behind its unreturning line,*
> *The vanished hour, no longer thine:*
> *One hour alone is in thy hands,—*
> *The NOW on which the shadow stands.*[1]

Yes, we should learn from the past, and yes, we should prepare for the future. But only *now* can we do. *Now* is the time we can learn. *Now* is the time we can repent. *Now* is the time we can bless others and "lift up the hands which hang down."[2] As Mormon counseled his son Moroni, "Let us labor diligently; . . . for we have a labor to perform [while] in this tabernacle of clay, that we may conquer the enemy of all righteousness, and rest our souls in the kingdom of God."[3]

The adversary never sleeps. There will always be opposition to

189

the truth. I repeat my urging from this morning to do those things that will increase your positive spiritual momentum, that lift Elder Dieter F. Uchtdorf was talking about, that will keep you moving forward through whatever challenges and opportunities come.

Positive spiritual momentum increases as we worship in the temple and grow in our understanding of the magnificent breadth and depth of the blessings we receive there. I plead with you to counter worldly ways by focusing on the eternal blessings of the temple. Your time there brings blessings for eternity.

As the Church grows, we strive to keep pace by building more temples. Forty-four new temples are presently under construction. More are being renewed. I pray for the skilled people who work on those projects across the world.

In the spirit of prayerful gratitude, I am pleased to announce our plans to build a new temple in each of the following locations: Wellington, New Zealand; Brazzaville, Republic of the Congo; Barcelona, Spain; Birmingham, United Kingdom; Cusco, Peru; Maceió, Brazil; Santos, Brazil; San Luis Potosí, Mexico; Mexico City Benemérito, Mexico; Tampa, Florida; Knoxville, Tennessee; Cleveland, Ohio; Wichita, Kansas; Austin, Texas; Missoula, Montana; Montpelier, Idaho; and Modesto, California.

These 17 temples will bless countless lives on both sides of the veil. I love you, my dear brothers and sisters. More important, the Lord loves you. He is your Savior and your Redeemer. He leads and guides His Church. May we be a people worthy of the Lord, who said, "Ye shall be my people, and I will be your God."[4]

For this I pray in the sacred name of Jesus Christ, amen.

Notes

1. Henry Van Dyke, "The Sun-Dial at Wells College," *Music and Other Poems* (1904), 116.
2. Hebrews 12:12.
3. Moroni 9:6.
4. Jeremiah 30:22.